On Message Structure

On Message Structure

A framework for the study of language and communication

R. Rommetveit

*Institute of Psychology,
University of Oslo*

A Wiley–Interscience Publication

JOHN WILEY & SONS

London · New York · Sydney · Toronto

Library of Congress Cataloging in Publication Data:

Rommetveit, Ragnar.
On message structure.

'A Wiley–Interscience publication.'
1. Languages—Psychology.   2. Communication.
I. Title.

P106.R56   401'.9   74–174

ISBN 0 471 73295 8

Printed in Great Britain by J. W. Arrowsmith Ltd.
Winterstoke Road, Bristol.

PREFACE

THIS BOOK deals with language, thought and human communication, and it is addressed to students of social sciences, humanities and philosophy who are seriously worried about the present fragmentation of knowledge into encapsulated fields of academic expertise. I am grateful to *the University of Oslo*, which has allowed me to devote full time to theoretical studies leading up to the present work, and I am greatly indebted to the *Netherlands Institute for Advanced Study in the Humanities and Social Studies* which, by inviting me as a fellow for 1972–73, offered the peace of the monastery combined with ample opportunity for stimulating interdisciplinary contacts.

December 1973 RAGNAR ROMMETVEIT

CONTENTS

I

INTRODUCTION

THE PRESENT work is in certain significant respects 'a cry from the wilderness'. Many of the ideas which were gradually elaborated into the notion of 'message structure' emerged during periods of isolation, some of them in a cottage in the Norwegian mountains, others in a house on the coast of western Norway, and still others on the beach of Wassenaar in the Netherlands. These different geographical locations served the very same purpose: that of prolonged detachment from busy university life and encapsulated academic dispute. In addition, they provided an optimal setting for pondering the question of *what remains true under conditions of silence* as compared to *what is claimed true under conditions of hectic debate within and between highly specialized academic subcultures.* Those who seek such insight into language and communication as can only be provided by the methodological and theoretical expertise of any such particular scientific subculture have hopefully been discouraged by the very subtitle of this work. If not, they may be frightened away by the following autobiographical confessions.

My first serious engagement (of an academic nature) in issues of communication and message structure dates back to the late forties, to seminars on symbolic logic at the University of Oslo. My teacher and friend, Professor Arne Naess, introduced me to the propositional calculus with its immanent elegance and power. Our joint attempts at recoding detective stories into propositional language, however, served at the same time as a very efficient antidote against formalistic escapism.

Subsequent studies of social norms and roles, ego psychology and social perception (Rommetveit 1953, 1958, 1960a) were all concerned with aspects of human communication. In my exploration of issues of complementarity in interpersonal relations I was strongly influenced by George Herbert Mead's symbolic interactionism, by Egon Brunswik's analysis of 'thing and medium', by Jean Piaget's theory of cognitive growth and decentration, and by Fritz Heider's work on attribution. Many of my social psychological studies seemed to converge in intriguing problems concerning interrelationships between language, action and thought (Rommetveit 1960b), and a series of experiments on the effects of verbalization on concept formation served as the empirical prelude to my psycholinguistic research during the last decade.

As to the theoretical prelude to the present work, perhaps the most important single aspect of it was my encounter with the very heterogeneous and

1

rapidly expanding field of psycholinguistics and structural linguistics in the United States. Through my reading and during my stays as a visiting professor at American universities I became acquainted with a variety of interesting approaches, such as the Illinois measurement of affective meaning and elaboration of mediation theory of meaning, the Johns Hopkins studies of associative word meaning and semantic–associative networks, the early Harvard application of information theory in exploration of sequential constraints, and the rapidly expanding Harvard–M.I.T. programme of psycholinguistics inspired by Chomsky's initial work on transformational grammar and subsequent ramifications into interpretative generative semantics.

When viewed against the background of my own as yet only vaguely elaborated philosophical and social psychological perspective, these approaches all carried promises of novel scientific avenues into particular aspects of language, thought and communication. Viewing them from some distance, however, I could not escape noticing definite symptoms of encapsulation, dogmatism and formalistic escapism. Thus, being greatly impressed and intrigued by the prospect of solving the riddles of the human mind via formal explication of linguistic competence, I was even more impressed by the optimism and the faith in their own self-sufficiency displayed by transformational grammarians and psycholinguists of the Harvard–M.I.T school.

A survey of the field of psycholinguistics in the United States in the late sixties left me with the impression of an intriguing and possibly insoluble puzzle. My search for some reasonable pattern in that puzzle resulted in a rather eclectic and open-ended representation of the entire field, although clearly flavoured by a characteristically European preoccupation with communication, contexts and subtle semantic issues (Rommetveit 1968a). Since then, further theoretical work of a more constructive nature has been inspired by such apparently divergent sources as Wittgenstein's *Philosophical Investigations*, Husserl's and Merleau-Ponty's phenomenological explorations, recent attempts at a dialogue between analytic and hermeneutic philosophers of language, studies of communication disorders by Gregory Bateson and co-workers, semiotic investigations by Lévi-Strauss, and even literary analysis by structuralists of the Prague school. Thus, while at the same time engaged in experimental research on word perception under conditions of binocular rivalry of letters, on cognitive strategies in Shannon-type guessing games, and on recall of utterances presented in pictorial contexts, my theoretical explorations led me all the way from the propositional calculus to poetry—with a profound disregard for traditional academic boundaries and barriers.

My first attempts at conveying fragments of the resultant conceptual framework to psycholinguists and linguists of the Harvard–M.I.T. school (Rommetveit 1972a, b) were met with reactions that convinced me that I had been trying to elaborate a paradigm differing from that of the prevailing school of thought in basic, yet so far only vaguely identified, ways. The chances of a fruitful dialogue with colleagues adhering to the prevailing school seemed indeed very slim. My most comprehensive and elaborate presentation of the proposed alternative paradigm was hence written in the Norwegian minority language and dedicated to Ludwig Wittgenstein, whose presumed spiritual support was of great comfort to me during my theoretical explorations (Rommetveit 1972c). The imagined alliance was perhaps facilitated by this physical context of my work: I was struggling to pursue Wittgenstein's basic ideas in terms of their implications for further inquiries of a linguistic and psycholinguistic nature, being surrounded by that very same western Norwegian silence to which Wittgenstein himself had resorted at times when pondering questions concerning in what sense and under which conditions something can be made known.

My early attempts at exploring subtle relationships between *communication settings, tacit presuppositions* and *what is said* were apparently interpreted as a rather esoteric activity—resembling Don Quixote's fight against non-existent obstacles and enemies—by linguists and psycholinguists focusing upon *the sentence in vacuo* as their basic clue to knowledge of linguistic competence and the human mind. Today, in view of the increasingly serious concern with tacit presuppositions *within* the Harvard–M.I.T. school, the scene is a different one. The leader of the school, Noam Chomsky, has thus within the last few years revised his assumptions concerning 'language essence' and 'language use'. His initial outlook, apparently shared by most of his followers in the fifties and early sixties, was expressed as follows (Chomsky 1968, p. 62):

If we hope to understand human language and the psychological capacities on which it rests, *we must first ask what it is, not how or for what purposes it is used.*

Four years later, however, he says (Chomsky 1972, p.198):

A central idea in much structural linguistics was *that the formal devices of language* should be studied independently of their use. *The earliest work* in transformational grammar took over a version of this thesis, as a *working hypothesis*. (Italics mine)

It is not at all unusual under conditions of crisis and revolution that what were previously presented as *dogmas*[1] are reinterpreted (and rebaptized) as *cautious working hypotheses*. What is of particular significance in the present context, however, is the actual expansion of inquiries into those areas of contextual and extralinguistic interrelationships which some years ago were considered taboo by many transformational linguists and psycholinguists. This makes it possible to try to show, more precisely and with reference to specific cases, how the approach proposed in the present work differs from the various extended and expanded versions of the Harvard–M.I.T. theory of language and mind. I shall therefore in what follows try to explicate the basic notions of message structure as a constructive alternative to the prevailing linguistic and psycholinguistic approach.

The most genuinely revolutionary aspect of the present work, however, is probably a Utopian search for a conceptual framework which may serve as a common basis for a whole variety of related, though at present academically entirely separated and encapsulated, disciplines. The ramification of what at one time constituted a global and vaguely defined topic for philosophical discourse into conceptually and methodologically encapsulated scientific disciplines seems to have reached its peak in subdivisions within psychology such as specialties like *non-verbal communication* and *studies of deep sentence structures.* 'Experts' from two such subdisciplines have today hardly any shared conceptual basis for a scientific dialogue. Nor can any of them engage in any scientifically meaningful discourse with a friend whose academic expertise pertains to, for example, *literary analysis.*

This is indeed a rather sad state of affairs, in particular if we keep in mind how the expert on sentence structures and his friend, the expert on poetry, prior to their academic specialization actually may have entered the same university with very similar, though only vaguely apprehended, objectives of deepening their understanding of the human mind and human communication. *Divide et impera* seems to be an essential aspect of scientific knowledge: ignorance can hardly be defeated at all until it can be split up and attacked by research workers who come to know more and more about successively more and more restricted parts or aspects of the entire, initially only vaguely defined field. It is doubtful, however, whether genuine insight follows from such victories unless the resultant fragments of knowledge can be integrated into a coherent picture of the entire field. Academic boundaries, as they exist today in the humanities and social sciences, are certainly *not* God-given barriers between mutually exclusive avenues to knowledge. Nor are they institutionalizations of basically different modes of knowing such as *understanding* ('*Verstehen*') as opposed to *explaining.* Some of them may upon closer examination actually betray symptoms of a deplorably secular genesis, such as the modern academician's needs for personal achievement and professional security within a narrowly defined field of academic competence *and* his institution's docile acceptance or even encouragement of those needs.

A confessed disrespect for existing boundaries between academic disciplines dealing with language, thought and human communication, however, does not imply lack of appreciation of the heterogeneity and complexities of the issues under investigation. The very idea of any common single and unitary conceptual framework is, in view of that heterogeneity and those complexities, a truly Utopian prospect. A Utopian idea, however, may serve as an impetus to action towards less Utopian goals, such as, in the present case, that of preparing the ground for more rewarding dialogues across existing academic boundaries.

II

PHILOSOPHICAL ASSUMPTIONS INHERENT IN CURRENT SEARCH FOR LATENT LANGUAGE STRUCTURE

A FUTURE historian of science will very likely reveal marked traces of a Platonic heritage in many current paradigms of humanistic and social scientific research, even within fields of inquiry in which prominent active researchers appear to be totally unaware of such heritage. A characteristic feature of current approaches to acts of verbal communication, for instance, is a tendency to spatialize and detemporalize events. This is not only true of *structural linguistics*, but also of general programmes for research in *psycholinguistics* whose proponents claim agnostic innocence and/or detached independence as far as any kind of philosophical heritage is concerned (Miller and McNeil 1969).

In addition to the tendency to spatialize and detemporalize—two distinctive features of our Platonic heritage, according to Bergson—we also witness symptoms of reification of aspects of events in terms of, for example, 'internal and external structures of sentences' (Bever 1970, p. 312), 'deep sentence structures' (Rommetveit 1972b), and 'underlying conceptual realities' (Fillmore 1972, p. 9). Such latent structures are identified as utterances are mapped on to (or interpreted as derivations from) underlying syntactic structures or abstract expressions of a semi-propositional nature. *What people actually say* is hence often relegated from the Platonic universe of *what can be said by 'the idealized speaker–hearer'*.

Mortals whose linguistic performance is thus condemned may be comforted, however. Their deviance may at times actually testify to 'metaphorical' or even 'poetic' exceptions to the basic latent rules, i.e. to a competence within the (undefined) Platonic domain of language use which even allows the native speaker to transcend that domain—and hence also allows him to play tricks upon the linguist in search of his basic competence. Moreover, segments of what is said and understood (such as words) are mapped on to hypothetical lexica, and the outcome is as a rule most flattering to the fluent speaker–hearer. At a minimum, such lexica allow for inference from rather trivial segments of everyday discourse to very impressive conceptual capacities. At a maximum,

5

they assign to the generalized speaker–hearer a latent knowledge of the world equal to that of the entire scientific heritage of his society. A technically unsophisticated person who is allowed to look up the entry for, for example, the word 'carburettor' in such a lexicon, for instance, will thus be genuinely impressed at the neo-Platonic wisdom he has intuitively displayed every time he has spoken that word.

But he may also—as the native speaker–hearer whose intuitions are assumed to be revealed in such Platonic grammars—become suspicious of the entire academic enterprise. Those who praise his intuition the most show in fact a negligible interest in *what he actually says* and *how, by what he says, he manages to make something known to others*. His intuitive mastery of the language can only be exhibited under conditions of constantly changing extralinguistic settings and interpersonal relations and hence, of course, in intricate interplay with a variety of other capacities. But the scholar in search of latent language structure tries to detach the intuition of the native speaker–hearer from the 'stream of life' in which it is embedded and, by expropriating it, makes it the major empirical legitimization of a twentieth-century scholastics.

As a consequence, a rapidly increasing number of scholars have become engaged in an increasingly complicated and formalistic exegesis of sentences *in vacuo*. A major proportion of the latter are made up by the linguist or the psycholinguist in his armchair, the most queer ones very often for the purpose of settling some internal controversy with respect to parsimony of formal representation and/or options of axiomatization. A current controversy within transformational grammar thus concerns the question of whether the postulate of a distinctive 'deep syntactic structure' should be replaced by a presumedly different postulate concerning 'logical form' inherent in 'surface structure' (see Lakoff 1972, p. 553, and Chomsky 1972, in particular pp. 72 and 139).

Increasing complexity and internal controversies within a semi-formalized system of ideas may sometimes initiate chain reactions, the final outcome of which may be such as to shake the very foundation of the entire system. What appears to be a controversy concerning options of axiomatization, for instance, may develop into controversies revealing divergent tacit presuppositions concerning the nature of syntactic structure, formal logic and 'nature logic'. Such divergencies may in turn betray different, though as yet only very vaguely indicated, views with respect to the ultimate goal of current search for latent language structure and the rationale for particular strategies of axiomatization. Which interrelationships, for instance, are assumed to exist *a priori* between the (expropriated) intuition of the native speaker–hearer, samples of his actual linguistic performance and formal logic? What, precisely, is achieved by mapping segments of discourse on to expressions of a semi-propositional form?

The various versions of the propositional calculus are dialects of an artificially created language. The latter was developed for particular purposes, and with carefully calculated gains and costs: by postulating atomic entities (propositions) whose truth values could be unequivocally assessed *and* remained invariant across combinatorial contexts, *an algorithm for assessing truth values of composite expressions was gained at the cost of the inherent flexibility of natural language.* Thus, perfectly legitimate and comprehensible segments of everyday discourse may be shown to be contradictory when evaluated in terms of propositional attributes and gauged against the criteria of formal logic. To label such segments 'ungrammatical' is certainly a novel and somewhat esoteric practice (see, for instance, Katz and Fodor 1963, p. 200). The observation itself should hardly be a surprise at all, however, certainly not to those who are familiar with the development of formal logic. Thus Quine writes (1972, p. 451):

> No one wants to say that the binomials of Linnaeus or the fourth dimension of Einstein or the binary code of the computer were somehow implicit in ordinary language, and I have seen no more reason to so regard the quantifiers and the truth functions.

A documentation of particular shortcomings of natural language as gauged against the propositional calculus is thus, in view of the very genesis of the latter, a mere tautology; and resort to truth functions and related notions from formal logic in current research on latent language structure must obviously serve purposes other than such documentation. But which other purposes can be inferred from what proponents of the various branches of the Harvard–M.I.T. school of scholars say and do with respect to the purely formalistic aspects of their trade?

In an attempt at exploring this issue, I have earlier (Rommetveit 1972a, pp. 240–45) tried to disentangle a purely *technical–derivational aspect* from *aspects concerning semantic content* in Chomsky's initial formal representations of syntactic structures. Pursuing this dichotomy further, one may even try to disentangle 'harmless' formal devices serving purely technical–derivational purposes from aspects of formalization with some inherent commitment of a theoretical nature. Consider, for instance, the task of establishing equivalence classes of sentences differing with respect to surface structure and that of identifying cases of syntactic ambiguity. Both these tasks can be performed by means of an algorithm defined exclusively in terms of formation and transformation rules, i.e. with a minimum of theoretical commitment and without any reference to the truth functions of the propositional calculus. The equivalence of 'Bill hit John' and 'John was hit by Bill' can simply be defined in terms of explicit rules of transformation. The ambiguity of 'They are flying planes' may be identified in terms of two distinctively different 'derivational histories'.

Subtle theoretical commitments seem to be involved, however, as soon as reference is made to 'readings' of sentences and to *synonymy salva veritate.* These commitments have to do with what I have previously labelled a tacit 'picture theory' of language use (Rommetveit 1972a, b), and they are becoming more and more visible as scholars of the Harvard–M.I.T. school expand their operations from *syntax* via *semantics* into linguistic and extralinguistic *presuppositions*, i.e. from explication of syntactic form to actual language use. Let us therefore first survey some programmatic statements by outstanding representatives of the school, and afterwards try to show how their common commitment to a picture theory is revealed in explication of 'readings' and criteria for synonymy in their analysis of specific sentences.

Chomsky's general philosophy of language is Cartesian: he is concerned with *linguistic performance* (in order to gain insight into *linguistic competence*), and linguistic competence is assumed to provide significant clues to *the mind*. Linguistics should hence be considered as a branch of cognitive psychology. As indicated in the Introduction, however, his view on issues of language essence and language use has obviously undergone some revision (see p. 3). His statements concerning interrelationships between cognitive capacities and linguistic competence, moreover, are remarkably ambiguous. Thus, having declared linguistics a branch of cognitive psychology, he writes (Chomsky 1968):

> (p. 53) We observe ... that knowledge of language ... is to a large extent *independent of intelligence* ...
> (p. 53, referring to empirist assumptions concerning language acquisition) They offer no way to describe or account for *the most characteristic and normal constructions of human intelligence*, such as linguistic competence.
> (p. 68, regarding the prospect of the generative grammar for some language as a clue to the origin of knowledge) What initial structure must be attributed to the mind ...? ... it appears to be *a species–specific capacity* that is essentially *independent of intelligence.* (Italics mine)

Issues of language and mind which remain open-ended and ambiguous when discussed in terms of linguistic competence and intelligence, however, are discussed by Lakoff in terms of assumed relationships between natural language and reasoning. He writes (Lakoff 1972):

> (p. 545) ... most reasoning that is done in the world, is done in natural language. And, correspondingly, most uses of natural language involve reasoning of some sort.
> (p. 559) Generative semantics claims that the underlying grammatical structure of a sentence *is* the logical form of that sentence.
> (p. 545) The notion of logical form is to be made sense in terms of a 'natural logic', a logic for natural language, whose goals are to express all concepts capable of being expressed in natural language, and to mesh with adequate descriptions of all natural languages.

Fillmore, on the other hand, is far more pessimistic concerning the prospect of disentangling the intricate interrelationships between language and thought, confessing (Fillmore 1972, p. 23), 'I ... frequently find myself speaking without understanding of what I am saying.' His actual semantic analysis, however, is replete with notions borrowed from the propositional calculus, and admittedly aimed at establishing some sort of isomorphy between semantic features of ordinary language and some Platonic universe of concepts. Consider, for instance, the following passages (Fillmore 1972):

> p. 7) Assuming that the *underlying semantic predicates* have their *argument slots* arranged in a fixed order, one can define *converse* relations between *predicates* in terms of *their underlying expressions* . . .
> (21-d) John sells roses to schoolgirls;
> (21-e) schoolgirls buy roses from John;
> (21-f) sell $\{a, b, c,\}$ = df buy $\{c, b, a\}$.
> (p. 9, concerning paraphrases of KILL, PERSUADE with CAUSE) The question is whether this reformulation is indeed significantly closer to *the underlying conceptual reality*! (Italics mine)

The task assigned to psychologists joining the Harvard–M.I.T. scholastics was at one time defined (Ervin-Tripp and Slobin 1966, p. 436) as that of '. . . finding the processes by which the competence described by the linguists is acquired by children and is reflected in performance under a variety of conditions'. This task has proved more and more futile as theories of linguistic competence have changed and become increasingly complicated. The faith in some form of psychological reality of at least *some* linguistic structures is sustained, however. Thus Bever, trying to cope with psychological aspects of language mastery in a world of rapidly changing linguistic theory, writes (Bever 1970):

> (p. 285, referring to people's capacity to distinguish between sentences and nonsensical strings of words, to identify syntactic ambiguity, etc.) All of these judgments require that the adult have *the concept of the language as a system independent of actual use* . . .
> (p. 286) The fact that every sentence has an internal and external structure is maintained by all linguistic theories—although the theories may differ as to the role the internal structure plays within the linguistic description. Thus *talking involves actively mapping internal structures into external sequences*, and understanding others involves *mapping external sequences into internal structures*. (Italics mine)

These scattered, though fairly representative, samples of programmatic statements may be surveyed with the objective of revealing some basic common philosophy of language underlying the various ramifications of the Harvard–M.I.T. school. The outcome is most unsatisfactory, however: what is shared seems to be *some faith in the orderliness of mind* and a presupposition, apparently contrary to Quine's expectation, that *natural language possesses some inherent logic of its own, a logic whose nature can only be revealed by continued investigations*. Lakoff, defining 'natural logic' as 'the empirical study of the nature of human language and human reasoning', also comments upon the time perspective of such investigations. The task of explicating 'all the relevant generalizations concerning the relation between logical forms and surface forms' is such that it 'would be ludicrous to think of . . . as accomplished within the next several centuries, if possible at all' (see Lakoff 1972, pp. 648 and 589).

Proselytes to such a grandiose scholastic movement must therefore have strong faith and a great tolerance of ambiguity with respect to the philosophical premises of the movement. How, for instance, shall we make sense of what Lakoff says about 'most reasoning that is done in the world' and his assertion that 'most uses of natural language involve reasoning of some sort'? Wittgenstein's philosophical investigations were to a considerable extent devoted to issues of language and thought. The outcome of his penetrating analysis, however, is clearly at variance with Lakoff's optimism: many of Wittgenstein's case studies show how we may be *seduced by 'the grammar of words'*, i.e. how logical stringency at times can only be achieved by emancipation of thought from ordinary language. His conclusions with respect to these basic issues were by no means merely impressionistic reflections, but also based upon careful calculation of gains and costs of formal emancipation from natural language in his earlier creative work in logic.

We may also wonder how Fillmore will be able to identify 'an underlying conceptual reality' if he should ever come across such an entity. At least three relatively 'pure' strategies may be considered. He may, first of all, try to derive (or construct) such an entity by paraphrasing and/or substitution and/or other purely intralinguistic procedures. He can hardly conceive of an entity derived by such intralinguistic analysis as an '*underlying* reality', however. Nor can he avoid, if we trust Wittgenstein's conclusions, being seduced by 'the grammar of the word'.

The next alternative then is to resort to the most advanced scientific lexica of relevance for the semantic feature under investigation. In the case of verbs such as 'sell' and 'buy', for instance, he may find out how the transactions referred to by the verbs are defined within sociology and/or economics and/or law. As indicated by the example, such an approach implies difficult and apparently arbitrary decisions concerning which one of a set of alternative scientific representations should be chosen as 'the underlying conceptual reality'. And any 'reality' arrived at by such procedures will necessarily, by definition, belong to a neo-Platonic universe of concepts *above* the intuition, linguistic or non-linguistic, of any native speaker–hearer who has not been scientifically trained in that particular discipline.

A third possibility is to resort to psychological inquiries into categorization and concept formation, i.e. to examine what people actually do when discriminating between different composite events and how particular aspects of such events are attributed to invariant and/or recurrent features of their entire 'Lebenswelt'—including other people and themselves. This strategy has been advocated by Chafe (1970, p. 75), who argues that practice in the discrimination of concepts should be considered as essential a part of the training in linguistics as practice in the discrimination of sound. Thus, 'semantic markers' whose epistemological status appeared to be a hybrid of *Kant's a priori* and *advanced scientific knowledge* (see Katz and Fodor 1963) may be replaced by underlying entities of a far less Platonic (and epistemologically more simple) nature.

This avenue seems very promising, but also extremely difficult, though some of the difficulties have already been identified and explored quite extensively within cognitive psychology. Consider, first of all, some empirical psychological evidence related to Wittgenstein's stimulating reflections concerning *to know* and *to say* (Wittgenstein 1968, p. 36). Experiments on concept formation, concept attainment and categorization have shown quite convincingly that people may know something without being able to put it into words (see Hull 1920, Hebb 1946, Rommetveit and Kvale 1965). Neither experimental demonstrations of such 'functional concepts' nor observations of pre-linguistic strategies of categorization in children should surprise linguists of the Harvard–M.I.T. school: there is *a priori* no reason to believe that Man's knowledge of the language he is speaking is any more intuitive than, for example, his knowledge of the interpersonal transactions in which he is engaged. But if his actual categorization of events also is of a truly intuitive nature, how can it then be assessed as the underlying conceptual reality against which Fillmore's paraphrases of words are to be validated?

A survey of empirical psychological research bearing upon the relationship between conceptual mastery and verbal labelling provides us with a picture of scattered and incomplete, though rather illuminating, evidence. The interrelationships seem, indeed, to be of a highly varied and intricate nature. In the field of categorization of interpersonal transactions, for instance, words may at times apparently even serve as socially appropriate camouflage of intuitively established perceptual and conceptual strategies. Inquiries into conceptual mastery of some aspects of the 'physical' world, on the other hand, testify to subtle and as yet only poorly understood transformations of pre-linguistic strategies of categorization into linguistically structured conceptual mastery (see Rommetveit 1972c, pp. 226–62).

A linguist in search of *psychological* 'realities' underlying semantic features of natural language will thus have to join the psychologist in a joint venture. The psychologist can certainly *not* provide him with anything resembling a ready-made repertoire of underlying realities in terms of concepts, categories or features of events. Nor can he offer him a handbook for practice in discrimination of concepts. The linguist and the psychologist, however, may together pursue some very promising paths of exploration, such as Michotte's early experimental investigations of phenomenal causality (Michotte 1954), Heider's subsequent analysis of personal versus impersonal causality and penetrating explorations of systems of attribution inherent in intuitively mastered human interaction (Heider 1958), and Piaget's thorough and extensive investigations of decentration and development of cognitive operations (Piaget 1952). These are, indeed, paths to which I shall repeatedly return in subsequent attempts at explicating message structure and the temporarily shared social reality of the dialogue.

Let us at this stage, however, turn to assumptions concerning division of labour between linguists and psychologists inherent in the Harvard–M.I.T. approach and, more specifically, to Fillmore's and Bever's programmatic statements. The latter are remarkable in two important and related respects: they are both clearly coached in the 'naive realism', as opposed to the 'constructivism' style of modern structuralism (see Piaget 1968), and they testify to great mutual faith. Thus, Fillmore seems to be convinced that he is not merely chasing shadows by assuming that variant, and at times shadow-like, occurrences of some semantic structure have as their common source some psychologically defined and invariant conceptual reality. Bever, on the other hand, believes that every sentence has at least some linguistically defined internal structure, though he does not even attempt to define or assess the conceptual reality presumedly required in order to validate it. Instead of an explicit programme for cooperation and division of labour, we thus encounter a very strange epistemological game of hide-and-seek in a world of shadows and assumed, respectively psychological and linguistic, realities. The sum of faiths seems to remain remarkably constant over time, however: as faith in *the psychological realities of linguistic structures* is reduced, faith in *the linguistic relevance of undefined psychological realities* is increased.

The formalistic escapism inherent in the game becomes even more transparent in Bever's presumably psychological account of *talking* and *understanding*. It is, of course, perfectly legitimate for a psycholinguist to formulate some formal constraints with respect to research strategy such as, for example, a commitment to explicate what is said in terms of external and internal sentence structures. As long as he believes in the existence of such structures but is admittedly ignorant with respect to their exact nature, however, he must envisage severe difficulties in his actual research as he is going to map one such particular structure on to the other. His claim that talking and understanding involve such mapping simply makes it clear that he is not going to abandon the particular structural analysis he has proposed, despite the difficulties he can foresee. His account of what is involved in talking and understanding is thus, apart from what might be implied by his persistent faith, entirely content-free as far as the psychology of talking and understanding is concerned.

Another remarkable feature of Bever's programmatic outlook—in particular when viewed against the background of Chomsky's recently expressed caution (see p. 3)—is his sustained conviction that adults have the concept of language as a system independent of actual use. This conviction rests upon firmly established evidence showing that people are able to distinguish between sentences and nonsensical strings of words and to identify syntactic ambiguities. According to Bever (1970, p. 281), '. . . adult linguistic ability includes the ability . . . to *produce intuitions* about sentences' (italics mine).

Having been engaged for some years in experimental research with the explicit objective of exploring so-called intuitive cognitive processes (see Rommetveit 1960a, b, Rommetveit and Kvale 1965), I fail to see how the kind of judgments to which Bever refers can be said to reveal any intuitive capacity detached from language use. Production of intuitions, if ever observed at all *in vacuo*, was to my knowledge never so labelled until the native speaker–hearer, and his intuition, was expropriated within the Harvard–M.I.T. school. Let us therefore examine his productive service to the linguist and psycholinguist in some more detail.

His task is to pass judgments on segments of speech or written texts, and his employer provides him with no information concerning particular contexts for the segments he is going to judge. Comparing pairs of isolated sequences of words such as 'He kicked the can' *versus* 'Can the kicked he', he is able then immediately to pass judgment as to which one of the two is meaningful and which one is nonsensical. Similarly, many meaningful sequences—some of them, however, only with difficulty and after considerable deliberation—are recognized as ambiguous in characteristically different ways. Examples of such ambiguous sentences are 'He read carefully prepared papers' and 'The missionary is ready to eat' (Bever 1970, p. 285). Still other sequences, such as 'Sleepless green ideas sleep furiously' and 'I bought sincerity a grief ago' tend to be judged as belonging to the 'Can-the-kicked-he' category, i.e. as nonsensical or anomalous.

In view of the systematic methodology developed within psychology of judgment, the most characteristic feature of judgments such as those indicated above is their inherent ambiguity. In order to assess 'intuition', the researcher must of course take care *not* to specify what is to be judged in technical terms. The nature of the task hence remains 'intuitive' in the sense that it is not explicitly defined, but has to be inferred in a subtle interplay of presuppositions and expectations. Self-instructions on the part of the informant will vary with respect to important but vaguely apprehended issues such as what ability is being tested and what kind of discourse is being presupposed. *What* is being judged will accordingly vary, depending upon what the informant thinks the researcher expects him to do and upon the particular combination of verbal materials to be judged. Thus, the sentence 'My spinster aunt is an infant' may be judged as *nonsensical* (i.e. 'illogical') or *meaningful* (i.e. 'reasonable, can certainly be said'), depending upon whether it is judged in the immediate judgmental context of 'Parents are older than their children' or, for example, 'Sleepless green ideas sleep furiously.' In the same way, the sentence 'I bought sincerity a grief ago' may appear nonsensical when compared to 'He kicked the can', yet beautifully meaningful when compared to many actual excerpts from modern poetry and judged on the tacit presupposition of a poetic context.

The tacit and intuitive aspects of the judgments thus seem to be intimately related to actual and potential use, and to lack of specification of different domains of use: judging a sequence of words as *nonsensical* simply implies asserting that it *cannot be used*, and discovering *ambiguities* implies envisaging distinctively *different ways in which some meaningful sequence can be used*. By far the most comprehensible criterion in the case of illiterate informants appears indeed to be use, i.e. whether and under which conditions something can be said. They will also, unless forbidden to do so, spontaneously give reasons for their judgments in terms of descriptions of the kind of situations in which what they judge as meaningful can be said.

The linguistics and psycholinguistics of the sentence *in vacuo* resemble in some important respect the early psychological research on 'the nonsense syllable'. Ebbinghaus resorted to trigrams he believed to be nonsensical in order to study retention detached from meaningful connections. Linguists and psycholinguists all over the world have for more than a decade tried to assess linguistic competence, presumedly detached from actual use and intricate extralinguistic conditions, by presenting sentences *in vacuo*. What is left vacuous by the researcher, however, does not remain so when the informant or the experimental subject enters the stage. Trigrams that were believed to be nonsensical were made meaningful by subjects relating them to words, and are now employed in research with empirically established indices of 'meaningfulness' attached to them (Noble 1952). Research on recall of utterances *in vacuo* (Blakar and Rommetveit 1974) and explication of the conditions under which judgments of isolated sentences are made, moreover, indicate how the informant spontaneously resorts to potential uses and plausible contextual frames. The sentence detached from use is thus, like the nonsense of 'the nonsense syllable', *an experimenter-centred illusion.*

This opens up an entirely novel perspective on those sentences which have been judged as anomalous or nonsensical in some respect. Instead of accepting the judgment as a final verdict, passed by sacred intuition in abstinence from use, we may ask: what kind of discourse has been presupposed, and which tacit criteria of 'sense' have been induced by the linguist? What, for instance, is revealed about such 'intuitive' aspects of his trade when sentences such as 'My spinster aunt is an infant' and 'I bought sincerity a grief ago' are judged as anomalous?

A careful examination of these and a great variety of other rejected cases leaves us with little doubt: the domain of usage presupposed in the Harvard–M.I.T. school's judgment of 'grammaticalness' or 'sense' is simply propositional use, and judgments have been passed on propositional properties of sentences on the assumption that such properties can be assessed for sentences *in vacuo*. Thus, 'My spinster aunt is an infant' is anomalous in the sense that—assuming invariant and mutually irreconcilable truth values for 'spinster' and 'infant'—it can be interpreted as a composite and contradictory propositional expression. And 'I bought sincerity a grief ago' deviates from propositional norms in several ways: it will clearly be impossible to assess unequivocal truth values for sentences containing the word 'grief' if the latter is allowed to depict 'underlying conceptual realities' of either mood or temporal duration or both. Similar problems arise in connection with 'bought sincerity'.

In the absence of explicitly stated philosophical assumptions, we can thus nevertheless in retrospect distinguish a common core of philosophy of language. Lakoff's belief that 'most uses of natural language involve reasoning', Fillmore's assumption concerning 'underlying conceptual reality', and Bever's faith in autonomous internal sentence structures that can be assessed independent of actual use: these are fragments of *a picture theory of language* of essentially the same brand as that of Frege (1969), Russell (1940) and

Wittgenstein's *Tractatus* (1922), only far less explicitly formulated and possessing a remarkable lack of concern with the distinction between purely axiomatic components and respectively linguistic and psychological 'facts'.

By far the most significant recent development within the Harvard–M.I.T. school, as far as philosophy of language is concerned, is the expansion of scope of propositional analysis from the sentence *in vacuo* to the sentence in a context described in terms of presuppositions and propositional content. Thus, not all that is contained within the sentence is any longer interpreted as being asserted, but only part of it, its 'focus'. And this focus (i.e. what is asserted), it is admitted, depends upon what is presupposed. The revised scheme is hence presented by Chomsky as follows:

> (Chomsky 1972, p. 100) Each sentence . . . is associated with a class of pairs (F, P) where F is a focus and P a presupposition, each such pair corresponding to one possible interpretation.

Fillmore says about presuppositions:

> (Fillmore 1972, p. 21) Presupposing may be thought of as an act performed by the speaker in his production of the sentence or as an act *imputed by the speaker to one or more of the individuals whose properties or actions are described by the utterance* . . .
>
> . . . it should be possible to 'compute' the full semantic description of the sentence, including, of course, information about what its utterer must presuppose *to be true*, including its utterer's *imputations of presuppositions to individuals described or referred to in the sentence*. (Italics mine)

McCawley redefines 'semantic structure' so as to fit into the novel framework:

> (McCawley 1972, p. 542) A 'semantic structure' . . . will . . . specify not the 'meaning' of a sentence, but the 'content' of a token of a sentence, e.g., *It's raining* will have different 'content' depending upon when and where it is said.

And Lakoff, referring more explicitly to formal aspects of expanding the scope of analysis, writes:

> (Lakoff 1972, p. 587) An account of *the logical form* of a sentence must include an account of *the presupposition* of that sentence. (Italics mine)

Some rather subtle implications of this revised outlook will be explored more thoroughly in later sections of this work, in our attempts at analysing how something *is made known* by an utterance when it is nested on to a social reality, temporarily shared by the speaker and the hearer. What remains unchanged and shared across all recently developed expansions and ramifications of the Harvard–M.I.T. approach, however, is a primary concern with propositional form and content of what is said. And let us now examine how this sustained concern with truth functions and synonymy *salva veritate* is revealed in three recent samples of analysis from respectively Fillmore, Lakoff and Chomsky.

Consider, first, Fillmore's analysis of 'converse relations of predicates' (see p. 9):

(II A) John sells roses to schoolgirls.

(II B) Schoolgirls buy roses from John.

(II C) Sell $\{a, b, c\}$ = df. buy $\{c, b, a\}$.

Fillmore maintains that (II A) and (II B) are synonymous *salva veritate*: if (II A) is true, then (II B) must be true and vice versa. The two verbs BUY and SELL, though, make it possible (Fillmore 1972, p. 9) '... to speak of a buying/selling transaction from one of the participants' point of view ...'. In other words: (II A) and (II B) depict the same state of affairs or composite underlying conceptual reality, only depicted from different points of view. In yet other words: the two sentences are claimed to be strictly analogous to composite propositional expressions with identical truth functions, given any fixed set of truth values for a, b and c in (II C).

However, let us now explore what *may be made known* by (II A) in specific settings of interpersonal communication. Consider, for instance, the following situation.

John has been unemployed for some time, but was yesterday considering two possible jobs: he might start working as a picolo at Hotel Pheonix, or he might go into private business and have his own flower stand at the entrance of the new girls' college. Today, the wife of John's neighbour, meeting John's mother in the street, asks 'What is John doing?'. His mother answers 'John sells roses to schoolgirls'.

John had actually decided to do so, and he left early in the morning with roses and all the equipment for his flower stand. His mother is thus telling the truth, the whole truth and nothing but the truth. But she does *not* know whether any single schoolgirl has bought any single rose from John, nor has she made anything known as far as that question is concerned. What she had made known to the wife of the neighbour thus remains true even if schoolgirls do not buy roses from John.

The 'truth functions' of utterances such as (II A) in everyday life situations can thus clearly *not* be unequivocally assessed by Fillmore's analytic procedures. What is said about selling flowers to schoolgirls may, as in the case indicated above, serve to make known a choice between alternative jobs. And such functions can neither be explicated in terms of converse relationships between SELL and BUY, nor by singling out particular segments of (II A) as its 'focus' or 'propositional content'. Whatever is asserted by the answer 'John sells roses to schoolgirls' in the kind of situations indicated by our example must instead be assessed against the background of potential alternative answers such as 'John works as a picolo at Hotel Phoenix', i.e. in terms of *explicitly or tacitly established contracts concerning the topic of discourse*.

Consider, next, the following explication of synonymy by Lakoff (1972, p. 549):

(II D) I think Sam will smoke pot, if he can get it cheap.

(II E) If he can get it cheap, *then* I think Sam will smoke pot (= II D).

Again, we encounter a claim that two sentences are synonymous *salva veritate* by virtue of their semantic constituents and inherent propositional forms. But consider then the following not only plausible, but actually very probable, conversational context.

A married couple are sitting in their home all by themselves, brooding over their son, who for some time has indulged in conduct of which they both strongly disapprove. At a certain moment—noticing the gloomy expression and visibly exposed tension in her husband's face—the wife says 'What are you thinking about just now? What is worrying you, my dear?'. And he spontaneously replies 'I think Sam will smoke pot if he can get it cheap'.[2]

His wife's question clearly implies a proposal for a contract of some sort: an answer on *her* premises means a commitment on the part of her husband to tell what is his '*inner cogatio*' (Husserl 1962, p. 188) at that moment. What is *made known* by what he says must hence be assessed against the background of other potential and plausible answers such as *'I think Sam will never finish his university training', 'I am afraid Sam's girlfriend is pregnant', and 'I think of what will become of Sam when we have passed away.'* Sam's father will thus be lying to his wife if he anwers (II D), even though the brooding interrupted by his wife's question concerned, for example, the possibility that Sam's girl friend might be pregnant. The truth value of his '*if–then*' expression is in this context obviously of secondary relevance—if of any relevance at all.

The expression '*I think*' in (II D) in the particular context described above is thus a self-referring '*cogito*'. It cannot serve as a 'parenthetical verb' indicating, for example, subjective uncertainty with respect to an assertion or inference conveyed by the remaining part of the utterance. If his answer should be (II E), on the other hand, then 'I think' can no longer be interpreted as '*cogito*', but most plausibly as a parenthetical comment similar to 'I guess', 'I suppose', etc. (see Urmson 1963, p. 239, and Rommetveit 1968a, pp. 62–4).

Once more, we thus witness how an analysis of presumedly invariant semantic features and propositional form of *what is said* fails to capture significant differences with respect to *what may be made known*. Lakoff's analysis is basically of the same form as that of Fillmore, and its failure can be neatly described in terms of the gains-and-costs account of the propositional calculus: identical truth values are assigned to (II D) and (II E) on the very dubious assumption that the segment '*I think*', as far as semantic features are concerned, remains the same for the two sentences across different extra-linguistic conditions.

What is implied by the strict commitment to 'truth functions' in the Harvard–M.I.T. school is perhaps even more clearly revealed in a recent explication of 'readings' or 'semantic representations' by Chomsky. He compares the following three expressions:

(II F) John's uncle.

(II G) The person who is the brother of John's mother or father or the husband of the sister of John's mother or father.

(II H) The person who is the son of one of John's grandparents or the husband of a daughter of one of John's grandparents, but is not his father. And he maintains:

(Chomsky 1972, p. 85) If the concept of 'semantic representation' ('reading') is to play any role at all in linguistic theory, then these three expressions must have the same semantic representation.

This conclusion is remarkable in several respects. Consider, first of all, what happens if (II F) is replaced by either (II G) or (II H) in a sentence such as 'He always treated John as if he were John's uncle'. It follows from Chomsky's claim that any usage of the expression 'John's uncle' in that sentence beyond what is captured by (II G) and (II H) is simply relegated from the domain of usage for which the Harvard–M.I.T. school's analysis is assumed to be valid. And this might serve as a warning to scholars who express faith that Chomsky's explication of linguistic competence may prove useful even in *analysis of poetry* (see Bierwisch 1971, pp. 189 and 193).

It can be shown, moreover, that far more serious issues are at stake than the relegation of esoteric metaphors from some presumedly 'normal' yet unde- fined, domain of usage. Thus, according to Chomsky's explication, we are not allowed to call the lover of John's aunt (who has been living with her as long as John can remember) 'John's uncle' unless the two of them constitute a married couple. This may prove embarrassing to John, who indeed may consider that person his nicest uncle. It may also prove embarrassing to anthropologists who are sceptical towards particular bourgeoisie reifications of kinship systems. Thus, Lévi-Strauss argues:

(Lévi-Strauss 1964, p. 50) A kinship system does not consist of objective ties of descent or of given degrees of consanguinity among individuals; it exists only in the consciousness of men, it is an arbitrary system of representations, not the spontaneous development of a situation of fact.

Thirdly, we may examine the three expressions (II F), (II G) and (II H) in terms of potential differential presuppositions in accordance with Chomsky's claim that they are synonymous and his own formula for an expanded approach. John's uncle may, for instance, have been put in jail for drunken driving. John and his six-year-old friends have heard rumours that the misdeed was done by some relative of John, and they ask John's mother 'Who is that man?'. She replies 'He is the person who is the son of one of John's grandparents or the husband of a daughter of one of John's grandparents, but is not his father'. Her reply has, according to Chomsky's analysis, exactly the same truth value as the one she decided *not* to give, namely, 'He is John's uncle'. The latter would have been immediately comprehended by the six-year-old interrogators, however, whereas the reply she actually gave probably leaves them with the impression that some unknown, very remote relative of John did the drunken driving.

John's mother has thus managed to tell 'the truth, the whole truth, and nothing but the truth' without making known to the children that the man was John's uncle. And she may have done so by carefully gauging her words against a veridical presupposition concerning the children's conceptual and terminological mastery of kinship relations. Chomsky's explications of expressions such as 'John's uncle', while blatantly inappropriate in analysis of many kinds of everyday usage, may thus certainly be exploited for the purpose of uttering evasive truths.

The very complex issue of presuppositions will be discussed at some length in subsequent chapters and we shall then try to relate the way in which Chomsky and generative semanticists approach the problems to a proposed alternative. What hopefully has been achieved by the preceding analysis is some documentation of the need for an alternative approach, despite the recent expansion of scope within the Harvard–M.I.T. school. Common to all expanded and extended versions of interpretative and generative semantics is the request for unequivocal criteria for determining truth values of what is being said. Such criteria can only be established by adventurous assumptions concerning a *finite and already known universe of 'conceptual realities'* of some sort, against which the 'real' or 'underlying' meanings of words such as BUY, SELL, THINK and UNCLE can be validated. Such a universe—whatever its epistemological foundation might be—is then imposed upon acts of speech, and what is said can hence be described as true or false representations of composite nonlinguistic states of affairs. Algorithms for explicating 'readings' of sentences are gained at the cost of committing the most gigantic 'experimenter-centred fallacy' in the history of modern humanistic and social sciences. In the case of poor John who names the unmarried lover of his aunt 'uncle', and in the case of the evasive reply of John's mother, we end up with the queer scientific insight that John has engaged in deviant and his mother in proper language use.

But this is exactly what Wittgenstein realized might happen when in his *Philosophical Investigations* he refuted a 'picture theory of language' and rejected all versions of such a theory as foundations for analysis of natural language. The idea of *language as depicting reality* may, of course, serve as an ideal for scientific language: the scholar may try to maximize internal consistency within his scientific discourse by imposing carefully elaborated constraints upon words to be used as 'technical terms', disentangling them from the fluctuating extralinguistic conditions and variant subjective presuppositions of everyday language. Thus, divergent theories may be compared *qua* alternative 'pictures' of the same set of events, and commonly accepted rules of documentation and/or procedures for falsification may provide a basis for deciding which 'picture' yields the best representation of some restricted set of states of affairs ('*Tatsachen*'). Depicting, however, necessarily implies a severe restriction of potential perspectives. Some of the possible perspectives on *buying* and *thinking* inherent in the words BUY and THINK are thus deliberately sacrificed when the two words are adopted as 'technical terms' within, for example, respectively scholarly legal discourse and some area of academic cognitive psychology. Such 'scientific dialects' may in turn over time infiltrate nonscientific everyday language in subtle and as yet unexplored ways.

However, even the most highly developed 'scientific dialect' remains semantically open and potentially creative, and its emancipation from nonscientific ordinary language is only partial. Moreover, its semantic structure (particularly as far as truth functions are concerned) can hardly be disentangled from institutionalized and often technically very complicated procedures for establishing relevant empirical evidence and making professional decisions. Thus, Kuhn (1970) in his survey of interesting epochs of change within some of the natural sciences has shown how scientific language is embedded in tradition-bound scientific activity. Aubert (1958) has revealed how states of affairs representing social deviance of a marginal kind will be portrayed in distinctively different ways, either as 'crime' or as 'sickness', depending upon which one of two institutions takes charge of the case and which one of two different institutionally anchored professional terminologies are employed in describing it. Wittenstein's claim that an utterance has meaning only in the stream of life seems thus to hold true even for scientific and professional language (see Malcolm 1967, p. 93). And this may indeed serve as a consolation when we also in our scientific discourse, in particular in programmatic statements such as the quotations from Chomsky, pages 3 and 8, sin against the commandment about invariance of word meaning across different contexts.

III

IN SEARCH OF AN ALTERNATIVE POINT OF DEPARTURE

WHAT EMERGES as semantic structure in transformational grammar is obviously gained at the cost of relegating important aspects and significant potentialities of *use*. But what is the constructive alternative to such an approach? How is it possible to engage in any scientific inquiry into language, thought and communication without committing oneself to some form of picture theory of language and the severe gains-and-costs account of the propositional calculus?

Let us at first briefly consider instances when what is actually said or written appears to be ungrammatical, anomalous, or even contradictory. Consider, for instance, Dylan Thomas' expression 'a grief ago' (see Levin 1971, p. 183). The latter may be compared to far more conventional, but similar, expressions such as 'some time ago', 'a while back', 'a year ago', and others. And a verdict of anomaly has already been passed on it—in the name of the intuition of the native speaker–hearer—when the expression appeared under disguise in a sample of strings of words evaluated in terms of the Harvard–M.I.T. criteria for basic linguistic competence (see p. 13).

The criteria applied in most cases of literary analysis, however, appear to be of an entirely different nature: what is labelled 'anomaly' by the structural linguist may indeed by the student of poetry be praised as *creative transcendence of conventional use*. Thus, scholars having been trained to explore the intuition of the creative speaker or writer examine what is said or written with aims and presuppositions strikingly different from the philosophical assumptions inherent in the Harvard–M.I.T. theories of semantic structure. What is conveyed by the artist is in literary analysis *not* assessed by mapping his text on to algorithmically derived constellations of semantic features drawn from a finite universe of 'conceptual realities'. On the contrary: the artist's achievement is often evaluated in terms of his capacity to create novel social realities, i.e. to make the reader experience aspects of life which somehow appear to be blurred or even concealed in conventional language use. His task may even be defined as a genuinely paradoxical undertaking: he is committed to reveal, by means of words, what has become invisible as a result of conventional verbalization.

The expression 'a grief ago' is thus anomalous when gauged against conventional usages such as 'he has a grief' and 'a week ago', i.e. against

21

Platonic 'conceptual realities' of atemporal mood and pure, vacuous duration. What Dylan Thomas seems to have achieved, however, is a 'de-Platonization': *he has temporalized grief and 'emotionalized' duration*. Students of literature are often concerned with the dynamics of such achievements, for instance with questions concerning which activities are involved in creation and comprehension of poetry. Thus Lotman, exploring the aspect of 'play' inherent in literary art, maintains that the effect of such 'play' cannot be explained in terms of static co-existence of different 'senses'. He writes:

(Lotman 1971, p. 294) Every experience of a meaning constitutes a separate synchronic field, yet within it are contained the memory of antecedent and the consciousness of possible future senses.

What is conveyed by any particular segment of a literary text can as a rule only be fully understood in the light of preceding and/or subsequent segments. Text analysis thus implies serious concern with aspects of human communication which cannot be captured at all by the kind of linguistic analysis attributing atemporal semantic structures to sentences *in vacuo*. And creative transcendence of current conventional use, moreover, can upon closer examination most appropriately be described in terms of potentialities inherent in familiar usage: in the poetic expression from Dylan Thomas, 'grief' is apparently temporalized by the conventional pure duration of the 'a . . . ago' in which it is inserted.

The subjective and dynamic aspects of such creative transcendence constitute a topic of primary concern in existentialistic and phenomenological inquiries. Thus, Merleau-Ponty, trying to describe speaking and comprehending 'from within', writes

(Merleau-Ponty 1962, pp. 183–4) Thought and expression . . . are simultaneously constituted . . . In order that I may understand the words of another person, it is clear that his vocabulary and his syntax must be 'already known' to me. But that does not mean that words do their work by arousing in me 'representations' associated with them . . . Just as the sense-giving intention which has set in motion the other person's speech is not an explicit thought, but a certain lack which is asking to be made good, so my taking up of this intention is not a process of thinking on my part, but a synchronizing change of my own existence, a transformation of my being.

Merleau-Ponty's approach in the passage above differs from the Harvard–M.I.T. school of psycholinguistics in many respects. Apart from its existentialistic perspective and terminology, it emphasizes the complementary relationship of the speaker's 'sense-giving intention' and the hearer's 'taking up of this intention'. Thought and speech, moreover, are also explored as complementary activities. The search for 'the appropriate word' in order to make something known to somebody else may often, in authentic speech, actually serve to make that 'something' known to the speaker himself: the latter does not know precisely *what* he intended to say until he 'hits upon' some word or expression by which his thought can be completed. The moments of creation in creative writing may be conceived of as events when something—until that moment wordless and only vaguely intended—is made known by the very act of encoding it into words.

Psycholinguists of the Harvard–M.I.T. school were in their explorations of temporal organization of speech strongly influenced from the very beginning by Lashley's investigations of serial order in complex motor skills and by Chomsky's early theory of atemporal syntactic structures (see Lashley 1951, Chomsky 1957, Miller *et al.* 1960, Miller 1962). Psychologically, the deep syntactic structure of a given sentence might most plausibly be conceived of as some cognitive representation of its 'content' serving as the initial cognitive input to the encoding and reappearing as the final output of the decoding of that sentence. Speaking may then, in accordance with Lashley's general account of pre-integration of serially ordered behaviour, be described as an act of converting a cognitive representation which is in itself devoid of temporal order into a strictly temporally organized articulatory activity. And comprehending may be conceived of as the complex perceptual–cognitive activity by which the heard temporal sequence of speech sounds is converted back into atemporal cognitive content again. What is involved is thus, in Bever's terms, 'mapping internal structures into external structures', and *vice versa* (see p. 9).

Merleau-Ponty's phenomenological analysis represents an attempt at explicating aspects which are ignored and/or deliberately left out of consideration in such a model of speech and speech comprehension. Moments of creative transcendence are, according to Merleau-Ponty, by no means moments of deviation from ordinary language use. On the contrary: every instance of verbal communication is in some important respects creative. Initiating a dialogue, for instance, is to 'transform a certain kind of silence into speech' (Merleau-Ponty 1962, p. 184). Once the other person accepts the invitation to engage in the dialogue, his life situation is temporarily transformed. The two participants leave behind them whatever were their preoccupations at the moment when silence was transformed into speech. From that moment on, they become inhabitants of a partly shared social world, established and continuously modified by their acts of communication. By transcribing what they say into atemporal contents of utterances, moreover, we clearly disregard those dynamic and subjective aspects of their discourse which Merleau-Ponty seems to have in mind when referring to 'synchronizing change of . . . own existence' and 'transformation of . . . being'.

Merleau-Ponty provides us with no unequivocal conceptual framework for exploring the actual or presupposed initial commonality which makes a dialogue possible, however. He tries to shed light on what is involved in authentic human communication 'from within', i.e. in terms of the individual experiences and existential conditions of the 'I' actively engaged in the discourse. Subjective, creative and idiosyncratic aspects are consequently brought forward at the cost of that common code and those shared presuppositions which, paradoxically, seem to constitute the basis for the kind of restricted, conventional language use defined in terms of Harvard–M.I.T. criteria of 'grammaticalness' as well as for Dylan Thomas' poetic transcendence of such use. Turning to existentialistic theories in search of a constructive alternative to prevailing linguistic and psycholinguistic paradigms, we thus encounter a dilemma: the existentialists apparently '. . . préfèrent un sujet sans rationalité à une rationalité sans sujet' (Lévi-Strauss 1971, p. 164).

How, for instance, can we account for the immediate, intersubjectively established, *here-and-now* of even the most simple dialogue in terms of purely private experiences on the part of the two participants? *How is it possible for any kind of social reality to emerge out of an encounter between two different and entirely private worlds?* Strawson warns against consequences of a radical subjectivistic approach to these basic issues of human communication. He maintains:

(Strawson 1969, p. 30) A different . . . error is made by those who, very well aware that *here-and-now* provides a point of reference, yet suppose that 'here' and 'now' and 'this' and all such utterance-centered words refer to something private and personal to each individual user of them. They see how for each person at any moment there is on this basis a single spatio-temporal network; but see also that, on this basis, there are as many networks, as many worlds, as there are persons. Such philosophers deprive themselves of a public point of reference by making the point of reference private.

Strawson thus calls our attention to two radically different points of departure for studies of human communication, the public *versus* the private point of reference. In retrospect, both of them appear familiar. With their resort to 'underlying conceptual realities', generative and interpretative semantics of the Harvard–M.I.T. school clearly seek to establish some public point of reference. Merleau-Ponty's reference to 'synchronizing change of . . . own existence', on the other hand, has as its point of departure the private 'I' of the person actively engaged in human discourse. Common to both types of approach, moreover, is a search for some Archimedean point which, once established, is supposed to serve as the origo of a unitary conceptual framework.

Meanwhile, human beings manage to make things known to each other in the absence of such an Archimedean point of reference. Communication takes place in a pluralistic and constantly changing world, only temporarily and partially shared. What constitutes the *here-and-now* at any particular moment of any particular dialogue is hence never an entirely public affair: it cannot be captured in terms of 'conceptual realities' imposed upon the situation from the outside, independent of the presuppositions and situationally determined perspectives of the individual participants. Nor can it be adequately described in terms of the private and idiosyncratic experiences of those individual participants. Whatever is made known at any particular stage of the dialogue must in some way be nested on to what both participants at that moment already know or assume to be the case. Strawson's sketch of alternative points of departure for studies of human communication is thus in some respects inadequate, and obviously not exhaustive. By refuting his dichotomy we may hopefully pave our way towards a constructive third alternative: the *here-and-now* that constitutes the prerequisite for any human dialogue appears to be neither entirely public nor purely private, but has to be conceived of as *an intersubjectively established social reality*.

Let us now return to cases of so-called 'anomaly' and 'creative transcendence' of conventional use and examine some implications of such a type of approach. Consider, once more, the expression 'a grief ago'. There is obviously nothing particularly private and idiosyncratic nor unequivocally public inherent in the expression as such. When produced by a student learning English as a secondary language, it will immediately be met with negative sanctions on the part of his teacher. When that same teacher encounters the expression in the poem by Dylan Thomas, on the other hand, he may not only spontaneously accept it, but even admit that considerably more was conveyed to him by that very segment of the poetic text than by most other otherwise comparable, but more conventional segments. Moreover, what today is accepted as creative transcendence may in the future be adopted in successively more public and conventionalized use. And whatever happens to be conveyed by the expression in its poetic context can only be fully assessed in the light of that partly institutionalized poet-to-reader-of-poetry setting in which it is embedded—as opposed to a variety of other types of intersubjectively established settings in which it may appear.

In order to find out what is made known when something is read or heard we have therefore to inquire into what kind of contract has been established between the two participants in that particular act of communication. This implies, in turn, an exploration of which aspects of a multifaceted and pluralistic world constitute their temporarily shared social reality. Their dialogue may, for instance, by mutual and tacit agreement, be oriented towards aspects of social life such as temporary employment or choice of job, or they may tacitly have endorsed a contract concerning topic committing both of them to a temporary concern with profit and loss in business transactions. What is made known by the verb SELL in the utterance 'John sells roses to schoolgirls' will depend upon which one of the two, equally plausible and equally unequivocal, types of contracts has been endorsed at that particular stage of the discourse (see p. 16). And a similar reanalysis may be performed in connection with Lakoff's 'reading' of the expression I THINK (see p. 16). This expression may in the linguistic context of sentence (II D) under certain conditions form part of an utterance by which the speaker makes known his own mental preoccupation at that very moment. It may under other conditions—in sentence (II D) as well as in sentence (II E)—convey some subjective uncertainty with respect to the judgment he makes known by the remaining part of the utterance. And *what* is being made known may in either case be immediately comprehended by virtue of an unequivocally established 'sous-entendu du discours' (Ducrot 1972, p. 8).

Our critique of the Harvard–M.I.T. school can hence be rephrased in terms of a constructive, though as yet only vaguely suggested, alternative: its failure to account for even very familiar variations of everyday use can in part be traced to its tacit commitment to one and only one 'standard contract' for human discourse. What is implied by that 'standard contract', however, remains just as vague and undetermined as those 'underlying conceptual realities' against which 'readings of sentences' are supposed to be validated (see p. 19). As a consequence, deviations from such a 'standard contract' constitute an extremely heterogeneous set: some are simply 'ungrammatical' in the sense that they fail to conform to criteria borrowed from formal logic, others are 'semi-grammatical' deviations from literal use, and still others seem to represent transcendence of conventional use of a non-metaphorical nature.

What is judged an 'anomaly' from the point of view of a 'standard contract' for human discourse in a monistic universe of 'conceptual realities', however, may become entirely acceptable when examined in the light of entirely different philosophical assumptions. A pluralistic world is by definition a world of a great variety of alternative perspectives and strategies of cognitive categorization. Options of perspectives and categorization, moreover, are reflected in options with respect to contracts of communication. I may say about a particular person, for instance:

(III A) He is easy to please, or:

(III B) He has the capacity to gain pleasure from small things.

What I say may in either case be true, and the two sentences may even be synonymous *salva veritate*. Whatever 'conceptual realities' are involved in the two sentences, however, must be explored in terms of options of cognitive categorization and attribution, and neither sentence can be said to 'depict' the state of affairs referred to in its 'core' or 'kernel' linguistic form.

Let us assume that I am 'telling the truth', i.e. that by saying either (III A) or (III B) I in each case truthfully intend to make known what I have learned from the very same set of observations. By uttering (III A), I am then making known what I have observed by adopting a perspective conventionally associated with tasks. Inherent in what I say is thus a proposal for a contract, committing the listener and myself to conceive of pleasing that particular person as a task and hence to consider the person himself as part or aspect of that task. By uttering (III B), on the other hand, I am making known what I have observed by inviting the listener to join me in a presumedly very familiar cognitive strategy of attributing capacities to persons (Heider 1958).

Compare, now, sentence (III A) to a so-called 'semi-grammatical', metaphorical sentence such as:

(III C) He has become an instrument for his boss.

Whatever is being conveyed by such an utterance can apparently be made known if and only if the listener endorses its inherent contract concerning cognitive categorization: the 'He' referred to is to be conceived of as an entity used by the boss for the purpose of pursuing his own goals, an entity which in itself is considered devoid of control and intentions. Entities encountered at such purely instrumental loci of telelogical schemes are most often inanimate objects or devices. Indeed, a person as such is neither a task nor an instrument. Both sentence (III A) and sentence (III C) are hence instances of metaphorical use when gauged against a 'standard contract' for literal discourse in a monistic world of 'conceptual realities'. *A particular person may nevertheless be considered an aspect of a task as well as an instrument by virtue of conceptual potentialities and temporarily shared modes of categorization on the part of people thinking and talking about him.* Expressions such as 'is easy' and 'has become an instrument' must accordingly be explored in terms of different contracts concerning options of perspectives and cognitive categorization.

Sentences such as (III C) are traditionally discussed by linguists of the Harvard–M.I.T. school in terms of deviations from rules for literal use. Degree of 'grammaticalness' is then assessed by describing type and number of violations of so-called 'selection restrictions'. The anomaly of (III C), for instance, stems from a rule restricting the use of the word 'instrument' to inanimate entities only. Sentence (III A), on the other hand, is considered grammatical, since no such selection restriction has been assigned for literal use of the word 'easy'.

Problems of literal use, anomaly and creative transcendence of conventional use, however, appear in an entirely different light when approached on the assumption that human discourse takes place under conditions of temporarily shared social realities in a pluralistic world. What appears as an instance of violation of rules for discourse in a monistic universe of conceptual realities may indeed be conceived of as a manifestation of creative potentialities inherent in the everyday language of a pluralistic social world. The creative writer can make his reader experience previously unknown aspects of that world by no other means than semantic potentialities already available to the reader by virtue of the latter's intuitive mastery of everyday language. *Literary craftmanship must hence be explored in terms of the artist's mastery of the creative potentialities inherent in everyday language rather than as esoteric violations of rules for literal use.* Thus, Roman Jakobson maintains:

> (Jakobson 1966, p. 375) The poetic resources concealed in the morphological and syntactic structure of language, briefly the poetry of grammar, have been seldom known to critics and mostly disregarded by linguists but skillfully mastered by creative writers.

Metaphorical use may indeed be conceived of as particularly illuminating manifestations of the openness and creativity inherent in everyday language. And, as Cohen and Margalit argue:

> (Cohen and Margalit 1972, p. 724) . . . the novelty of a metaphor in speech no more constitutes an innovation in the language than the fact that a sentence has never been uttered before constitutes its utterance a product of syntactic change.

Consider, again, Dylan Thomas' expression 'a grief ago'. In what respect is the poetic emotionalization of duration conveyed by that expression different from, for example, the instrumentalization of a person conveyed by a conventional sentence such as 'He has become an instrument for his boss'? Imagine, moreover, a situation in which you are asked *how one particular person is*, and you answer either 'He is easy to please' or 'He has the capacity to gain pleasure from small things'. Let us assume that you have never verbalized your impression of the person until the very moment when you were asked about it. If so, in what respect is the moment you are uttering your answer different from moments during creative writing at which something previously wordless and only vaguely cognized is *made known* by the very act of encoding it into words?

Pursuing this question further, we may even explore the possibility that you may spontaneously answer (III A) or (III B), depending upon what constitutes '*le sous-entendu*' of the entire dialogue. Suppose, for instance, that your partner in the dialogue is seriously considering the possibility that he may offer a particular job to the person he is inquiring about. Being aware of that and knowing at the same time that the job is neither well paid nor particularly interesting, you may answer 'He is easy to please'. Imagine, on the other hand, a situation in which you know that the person you are asked about has decided to start out on a long and solitary expedition which in all likelihood will be very monotonous and devoid of exciting events. Assuming that your interrogator is worried concerning his ability to endure months of fairly uneventful travelling, moreover, you may answer 'He has the capacity to gain pleasure from small things'.

Of course, no one can predict what your particular answer will be in any one of the two situations suggested above. By pursuing the problem in such a fashion, however, we are forced to reflect upon genuinely creative and social aspects of acts of speech. Making known your impression of a particular person in particular situations such as those indicated above is clearly something more than converting a ready-made Cartesian cognitive representation into a temporally extended sequence of speech sounds. It is a social activity in the sense that you spontaneously monitor what you say in accordance with tacit assumptions concerning what both of you already know and what more your listener wants to know. You may thus induce a shared perspective by which the person you are talking about is considered a potential manipulandum, or you may engage your listener in a linguistically induced joint strategy of attributing talents to him. Moreover, whatever contract of categorization is established can only be induced by some creative combination of intuitively available semantic potentialities.

But what, more precisely, is meant by a social reality? What is implied by contracts of communication, and what are the relationships between such contracts, options of attribution and categorization, and the semantic potentialities inherent in everyday language use? And how can what is made known by an utterance be nested on to what is already presupposed in such a way that it becomes part of a temporarily expanded and/or modified social reality?

These are the issues we are now going to explore in some more detail.

IV

ON THE ARCHITECTURE OF INTER-SUBJECTIVITY

IV. 1. The Dialogue and the Temporarily Shared Social World

VYGOTSKY (1962) quotes a short passage from Tolstoy in which two people in love engaged in a dialogue consisting of initial segments of words and one-word utterances only, and yet 'understood each other perfectly'. Similar states of nearly perfect complementarity and synchronization of intentions and thoughts may also emerge out of far less romantic human conditions, for instance when a middle-aged married couple are temporarily united, not by the passion of young love, but by shared worries concerning their offspring. On such an occasion, an interrogatory gaze from the wife in response to the visibly exposed gloomy tension of her husband at that moment may serve as a prelude to the—to an outsider—very cryptic remark 'Pot'. And the wife 'understands perfectly': what is worrying her husband at that particular moment is the possibility that their son Sam may start smoking pot (see pp. 16–17).

Equally cryptic conversations may take place when workers are engaged in manual labour requiring cooperative interaction among them, and also when two persons are watching a football game together. Whatever is 'perfectly understood' under such conditions can only be assessed against the background of whatever constitutes the intersubjectively established social reality at the moment of the speech. By uttering 'Pot', for instance, Sam's father makes known to his wife neither more nor less than that which she does not already know, but wants to be informed about at that moment. And he does so because of what *he knows that she knows*, namely that he at that particular moment is immersed in worries concerning some aspect of Sam's conduct.

In accordance with Wittgenstein's suggestive metaphors about utterances as moves within different language games, embedded in streams of social life (Wittgenstein 1968)—and with some confidence in Tolstoy's intuitive insight into conditions of human communication—we may thus reverse the traditional linguistic approach to ellipsis: *ellipsis, we may claim, appears to be the prototype of verbal communication under ideal conditions of complete complementarity in an intersubjectively established, temporarily shared social world.* Full sentences—and even sequences of sentences—may be required in order to make something known, however, under conditions of deficient complementarity and less than perfect synchronization of intentions and thoughts.

29

Consider, for instance, two friends watching a football game together. At a particular moment, as both of them have been watching some exceptionally skilful manoeuvre, one of them exclaims 'That was magnificent!', or simply 'Magnificent!'. Consider, next, what he may have to say when they are on their way home in order to make known his admiration of that particular feat. What was veridically presupposed at the moment of his cryptic exclamation must now somehow be established by linguistic means, for instance by expressions such as 'That tackling performed by the slim, funny-looking quarterback . . .' or 'The manoeuvre which caused such a roar of acclamation towards the end of the game . . .'.

Let us, therefore, as a prelude to our explication of 'message structure', compare the following four utterances:

(IV A) Magnificent!

(IV B) That was magnificent!

(IV C) That tackling performed by the slim, funny-looking quarterback was magnificent!

(IV D) The manoeuvre that caused such a roar of acclamation towards the end of the game was magnificent!

Assuming that the cryptic exclamation (IV A) is triggered by what both friends have attended to in the football field immediately prior to the act of speech, we shall first of all explore what constitutes the linguistically relevant shared social reality at that moment. And we may do so simply by asking: what is implied by the 'That' of (IV B)?

Imagine, for instance, that the two friends are both real football fans: they both immediately comprehend what is happening in the field in terms of objectives, strategies, and discrete events such as 'tacklings', 'passes', 'touch-downs', etc. This implies, in turn, a shared strategy of categorization and segmentation. The object of admiration presupposed in (IV A) and conveyed by 'That' in (IV B) is thus a fairly unequivocal and immediately shared social reality by virtue of their convergent categorizations of the same—in itself very composite and multifaceted—visually experienced flow of events. As such an intersubjectively unequivocal entity, it may also be attended to retrospectively by both of them, and it may at some later time be brought to the foreground in a dialogue between them by expressions such as 'That tackling . . .' or 'The manoeuvre . . .'.

Each of the expanded utterances (IV C) and (IV D) can therefore be divided into two functionally distinctively different parts. The segment 'That tackling performed by the slim, funny-looking quarterback' in (IV C) serves exclusively as a bridge by which the linguistically mediated novel information is tagged on to an already established social reality. The same holds true for the first part of (IV D), i.e. of 'The manoeuvre that caused such a roar of acclamation towards the end of the game'. And the two segments are functionally equivalent in the situation of the dialogue after the game to the extent that either of them can be employed to induce a temporarily shared retroactive attendance to the very same tackling manoeuvre.

Whatever is intentionally made known by the identical second parts of (IV C) and (IV D) can only be made known and become part of an expanded shared social reality if such a shared attendance is induced. In order to make sure that he and his companion have the same entity in mind, the speaker may hence also deliberately check whether convergence on to the same social reality has been established before attempting to convey anything about his evaluation or admiration. The dialogue after the game may, for instance, proceed as follows:

'Do you remember that tackling performed by the slim, funny-looking quarterback?'

'The funny-looking quarterback?—I am not sure . . .'

'I am thinking of the manoeuvre that caused such a roar of acclamation towards the end of the game.'

'Oh yes, I remember that.'

'That was magnificent!'

In this case, convergent retrospective attendance to the linguistically relevant shared social reality has been established and confirmed only after some trial and error. The 'That' in the last utterance of the excerpt from the dialogue, however, appears to serve basically the same function as the 'That' in (IV B) when uttered while the two friends are both watching the game. As far as message structure is concerned, each such instance of 'That' must be conceived of as a bridge by virtue of which what is made known by the entire utterance becomes an expansion and/or modification of an already pre-established and presupposed shared social world. And none of the utterances (IV A), (IV B), (IV C) and (IV D) will make known to the listener *what* the speaker admires so much unless some such bridge to a common social world is temporarily established.

Imagine, next, a situation in which the man who was so impressed by that particular tackling manoeuvre is being engaged in discourse with another friend who is also a football fan, but who did not have the opportunity to watch that particular game. Retroactive attendance to an experientially pre-established social reality is hence prohibited, and some substitute for it must be achieved by means of other potential bridging constructions. The speaker, of course, spontaneously and veridically assumes that the listener and he—both of them football fans—have in common a fairly unequivocal and well-defined strategy for categorizing what goes on during a football game. He may perhaps also know the name of the slim, funny-looking quarterback, Bob Wilson. In that case, and knowing in addition that his listener too knows Bob Wilson by name as well as by sight and reputation, he may thus try to make known his enthusiasm for that particular historical tackling manoeuvre by saying:

(IV E) The tackling performed by Bob Wilson towards the end of the game was magnificent!

Of course, I shall not claim that (IV E) is *synonymous* with either one of the utterances (IV A), (IV B), (IV C) or (IV D). The 'deleted part' of (IV A), the 'That' of (IV B) and the parts preceding '. . . was magnificent' in (IV C), (IV D) and (IV E), however, may all be said to serve the function of 'identifying reference' (Strawson 1964). Making a temporary detour into the philosophy of propositions and truth values, moreover, we may even venture to claim that (IV A), (IV B), (IV C), (IV D) and (IV E), under the different kinds of extralinguistic conditions suggested above, may be conceived of as situationally and linguistically determined variants of one and the same assertion.

This claim may be further corroborated by a hypothetical expansion of the dialogue. The listener who has watched the game himself may, for instance, make known that he disagrees with or questions what has presumedly been asserted. It may even be possible to hit upon some device for settling the dispute: what, more precisely, is asserted by the word 'magnificent' may upon further discussion by consensus be defined as, for example, 'more skilful than the famous tackling manoeuvre performed by Bill Nelson in the Minnesota game'. And the Bob Wilson enthusiast may indeed be so stubborn (or so willing to be of service to philosophers) that he gets hold of authentic movies of the two games. In order to settle the dispute, he thereupon asks his two friends to watch both movies and judge which one of the two athletic feats was the more skilful.

His service to the philosopher of language is in this case considerable, even though he may fail to establish consensus with respect to the truth of what he has maintained. The philosophically significant aspect of the verification ritual thus does *not* pertain to the final verdict concerning truth value, but to the ease with which the object of his admiration is identified independently by each of the three judges. What by the two of them who have previously watched the real game together immediately is *recognized* as the referent of, for example, 'That' in (IV B) *or* 'The manoeuvre that caused such a roar . . .' in (IV D), is nearly as spontaneously *identified* as the referent of '*The tackling performed by Bob Wilson . . .*' in (IV E) by the football fan who has never seen that athletic feat before, but only heard about it.

By his elaborate verification ceremony, our Bob Wilson fan has thus done us a twofold service. He has, first of all, aided us in our deliberate efforts at transplanting a basic philosophical issue, traditionally encountered in a scholastic habitat of nonexistent unicorns and bald French kings, into a framework of everyday conversations. By examining the function of identifying reference within specific textures of social interaction, moreover, we have been able to show how alternative linguistic constructions may serve that very same function, depending upon what is already shared and/or veridically presupposed as shared knowledge on the part of both participants at that particular moment of their dialogue. The task of constructing a bridge from the *here-and-now* of the dialogue to some particular and unique event can hence not be solved by any publicly valid general recipe for 'identifying descriptions' (see Strawson 1964). Different constructions will be required depending upon what kind of foundations are available in the form of shared experience and strategies of categorization on the part of the participants in the dialogue. The bridge by which the novel information is linked to what was known beforehand and by which it thereby becomes part of an expanded or modified social world will in each case be exactly as fragile as the pre-established commonality between speaker and listener upon which it is founded.

Our observation that appropriate identifying reference is achieved in all cases, including the case of the listener who has not watched the game himself, is thus in some respect deceptive: it may tempt us to conclude that as much is conveyed to him as to the listener who has actually watched the tackling manoeuvre. But this is an entirely false conclusion. In one sense, *more* is made known to the person who has not watched the game, since he does not know of that tackling at all beforehand. In another sense, *less* is made known to him, since he—unlike the listener who watched the game—can neither endorse nor refute what is asserted by the speaker. The object of praise in utterance (IV B) is in fact only made known to him as a tackling performed by a football player he knows of, and performed towards the end of a particular game. It will hence remain only partially determined and identifiable only in principle until he is shown the film of the game.

Whether or not some entity is in principle identifiable became a crucial issue in scholastic philosophy. It is also an issue of primary concern in modern analytic philosophy, and in particular in attempts at assessing the conditions under which unequivocal truth values can be assigned to sentences. This problem may often be encountered in analysis of scientific discourse and verification procedures. Philosophers dealing with the function of identifying reference under such auspices habitually tend to conceive of reference in terms of an unequivocal dichotomy of success or failure, and they continue to do so even when dealing with sentences presumedly borrowed from contexts of nonscientific, ordinary discourse. Sentences such as (IV B), (IV C), (IV D) and (IV E) are then as a rule examined from the point of view of some hypothetical prospects of possible conditions of identification. If it can be shown that identifying reference can be established in one way or another, then a status as a potential proposition is ascribed to the sentence.

If, on the other hand, reference cannot be achieved under any conceivable condition of identification, a 'truth value gap' is apparently encountered (see Quine 1961, Strawson 1964). A sentence such as 'The present King of France is bald', for instance, can neither be true nor false since the referent of the expression 'The present King of France' simply cannot be identified at all. Such an expression must hence be sharply distinguished from formally similar descriptions such as, for example, 'The victor from Austerlitz', 'The loser in the battle at Leipzig' and 'The exiled emperor on St. Helena', all three of which are acceptable and even functionally equivalent when gauged against the dichotomy of success or failure of reference—since each of them under at least some conceivable set of conditions may serve to identify Napoleon Bonaparte.

The notion of an unequivocal dichotomy—being inherited from scholastic philosophy—appears to be *a sine qua non* if we venture to divide whatever can be talked about into 'real' and 'fictitious' entities in an epistemologically transparent universe. It may prove singularly awkward and even positively deceptive, however, if we consider it our task to explore what in the course of a dialogue is made known by one person to another in a world we assume to be multifaceted, only partially shared, and only fragmentarily known. The shortcomings of a dichotomous notion of reference may thus become particularly visible if we now, from our scholastic excursion to the realm of nonexistent kings, return to real-life situations of human communication and, more specifically, to particular educational situations in which a teacher tries to make known some historical event, to his students.

The teacher may certainly draw one important general conclusion from the scholastic notion of identifying reference: he should by all means in his descriptions of historical persons and events avoid 'truth value gaps'. In other words, he should take care never to describe nonexistent entities as if they were real. But even such an apparently simple and sound rule of thumb may become problematic, since different devices for communicating novel information concerning historical persons and events may be required depending upon which social realities are available as foundations on the part of his students in each particular educational situation. Consider, for instance, the task of teaching modern French history to illiterate adults in a tribal and secluded African community. The students enter the situation with hardly any preknowledge of Western societies and political systems at all. Whatever is going to be made known to them about modern France must hence be nested on to preconceptions established within their own restricted social world.

On such a difficult occasion, even a scholastic nonexistent French king may come in handy. The teacher may thus, for instance, deliberately violate his rule of thumb by refererring to the late President de Gaulle as 'the powerful king of France'. Thus, when a student asks him the question 'Who was that man de Gaulle?', his answer may be 'He was the powerful king of France'. The expression 'the powerful king of France' may subsequently in the dialogue be employed by the students as well as by the teacher as an 'identifying description' of de Gaulle. And the teacher's reason for employing that particular expression may be by no means malevolent or cynical: the fact may simply be that in that particular situation he can hit upon no better means of bridging the gap between what the students already know of relevance to the topic and what at such a stage of pre-knowledge can be made known to them about de Gaulle and his political role in France. What the teacher is telling them about a powerful king on that particular occasion is therefore actually wisely monitored in accordance with what he knows that they know.

What in a philosophical analysis of propositional attributes of sentences is encountered as an instance of a 'truth value gap' may thus in a particular educational dialogue constitute an ingenuous and even necessary didactic device. The crucial issue is in the latter case not an epistemological issue concerning real and fictitious entities, but has to do with the fact that President de Gaulle does not constitute part of the listener's pre-established social reality at all. He may become partially known, however, by means of descriptions such as 'the powerful king of France'. The expression may therefore be considered a metaphor: in order to make known what in literal (and Gallo-centric) words might be totally incomprehensible to them, the experienced teacher of history in fact invites his students to adopt a strategy of categorization they have already mastered within an experientially established and perhaps mythologically elaborated social world of tribal kings.

We have dealt with this situation at such length partly because it differs so markedly from the conditions of temporarily almost completely shared social worlds of Tolstoy's lovers, the middle-aged couple brooding over their son, and the two football fans watching a particular tackling manoeuvre. A dialogue between our history teacher and an African student of his about modern French history must in comparison be viewed as a genuinely creative and social activity of *constructing some sort of a bridge between very different and previously separate social worlds*. And whatever at any particular moment of that activity is being established as a temporarily shared social reality will necessarily be only partially shared and tagged on to pre-established knowledge by means of very fragile connections.

What at a certain stage of the dialogue has been made known to the student, moreover, cannot be fully assessed by finding out what he at that stage knows about *France* only. Even pre-established knowledge of parts of his own restricted world is bound to acquire novel dimensions in the light of what he gets to know about different and previously unknown ways of life. Such a modification of the student's outlook on his own contemporary society is not only supposed to take place in encounters with foreign cultures, but actually recognized and stated as an important objective in most programmes for general public education. The young generation is supposed to enrich its understanding of the present by learning about the past. And even French children enter their first history lessons with only fragments of knowledge of relevance to what is said in a classroom conversation in an elementary school about Napoleon and President de Gualle. Thus Napoleon Bonaparte's identity must for every new generation be re-established in dialogues between adults who have only partial knowledge of history and children who have none. He may in fact initially enter the child's experientially established social world of winning, losing and being rejected by virtue of metaphorical potentialities inherent in words such as 'victor', 'loser' and 'exiled'.

From our casuistic analysis we may now hopefully proceed to a more systematic explication and ask which significant general features can be distinguished across variant situational aspects of dialogues. What, for instance, is implied by presuppositions on the part of the speaker and the listener at the moment of the act of speech? How are such presuppositions related to their pre-established social worlds? In what sense, and how, are intersubjectively shared social realities established during and by virtue of what is said? How can components of commonality between different social worlds be accounted for in terms of partially shared strategies for categorization and linguistically mediated contracts concerning such strategies? What—if anything at all—is being made known under various conditions of temporary and only partially established intersubjectivity?

36

Let us, in order to pursue such questions in a somewhat systematic fashion, return to the *here-and-now* of the dialogue. Such a *here-and-now*, however, remains vacuous or at best only arbitrarily defined until the interpersonal speaker-to-listener coordinate of the act of speech has been determined as well. This follows from our refutation of either an entirely public or a purely private point of reference, and from our basic assumption that human communication takes place in a multifaceted, only fragmentarily known and only temporarily and partially shared social world. In order to explore all significant features of the partially shared social world of the dialogue, we need therefore at a minimum a system of coordinates such as the one indicated in Figure 1.

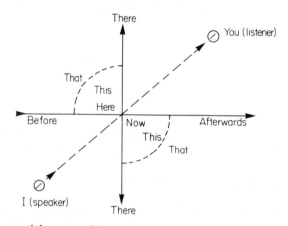

FIGURE 1. The spatial–temporal–interpersonal coordinates of the act of speech

The coordinates may in principle be defined in terms of the point in real *time* at which the act of communication takes place, its *location*, and (in the case of spoken language) the identification of *listener* by *speaker*, and *vice versa*. These coordinates cannot be fully assessed independently of each other and from the outside by, for example, a publicly unequivocal description of some particular location in space and real time and indices of public identities of the participants in the dialogue such as their proper names. The intersubjectively established *now*, for instance, will have very different denotative extensions depending upon what constitutes the topic of discourse. The *now* of the question from the wife to her worried husband is apparently a now at this very moment as opposed to, a minute or so ago. The *now* presupposed in an expression such as 'now in modern times' employed by either the teacher of history or his African student in their conversation about French political institutions, on the other hand, may encompass centuries. And the *here* presupposed in acts of speech during that dialogue may be here, in Africa as opposed to there, in Western Europe. In an entirely different setting, it may be here, from where we are watching that tackling as distinctively different from out there on the football field where that tackling takes place.

The *I* and *you*, moreover, are for any utterance of the dialogue immediately—and intersubjectively—given as a speaking I addressing a listening you, i.e. in terms of *an unequivocal direction of communication*. The listener must also, of course, be conceived of as an active I. What is made known to him may therefore, as indicated earlier, be explored even in terms of 'a synchronizing change of his own existence'. And we shall indeed in the next chapter return to some intricate philosophical issues encountered in such an approach when attempts are made to explore the actively engaged I and its relationships to a retrospectively reflected-upon me.

Let us at this stage, however, focus upon those aspects of the interpersonal coordinate of the act of communication which may possibly account for initial commonality and shared presuppositions. Which such aspects can be distinguished across variant situational settings, as recurrent and general features of the dialogue as such?

In retrospect, two intimately related features appear to demand our attention. We notice, first of all, how *some commonality is being established by the very fact that two persons engage in a dialogue*. The I and you constitute in every single case a temporarily established *we* engaged in that particular act of communication as opposed to *all others* (she, he, they) who are not so engaged. Whatever is shared, presupposed, or assumed as already known—even if in principle accessible to 'the public'—is hence something shared, presupposed or assumed by the speaker and the *us* within an intersubjectively defined *here-and-now*. Presupposing can therefore *not* be defined as 'an act imputed *by the speaker only—in vacuo* or "in public" '—as proposed by Fillmore. What is presupposed by the speaker must in each particular case be tagged on to the I–you coordinate of the act of communication, as *something that I, the speaker assume both of us (I and you) to know here-and-now*.

An equally recurrent and intimately related feature of the I–you coordinate has to do with the complementary relationship between speaking and listening, an aspect of the dialogue to be discussed more extensively in the next chapter. As far as presuppositions are concerned, however, complementarity can in part be conceived of as a reciprocally cognized asymmetry between I and you with respect to what is already known. What is said under certain optimal conditions of complementarity is thus monitored in accordance with veridical assumptions concerning what the listener at that moment does not yet know, but wants to know.

Consider, for instance, once more the case of the middle-aged couple brooding over their son, and the cryptic utterance 'Pot'. What is tacitly and veridically presupposed by the husband on that occasion must actually be conceived of as a sequence of assumptions, one nested on to the other. He knows, first of all, that his wife knows he is immersed in worries concerning some actual or potential misbehaviour on the part of their son Sam. Assuming that is the case, furthermore, he also assumes that she does not know which one of a range of such modes of delinquencies he has in mind at that moment. Her interrogatory gaze is on that basis spontaneously assumed to convey a quest for precisely that information.

The temporarily shared social world at any particular stage of a dialogue can thus be assessed only by explicit reference to the I–you coordinate of the act of communication, i.e. as that which I know that you know *and* you know that I know as well. Our three major variants of dialogues between football fans vary in that respect. What remains shared under all three sets of conditions, however, is a particular strategy of categorization by which something happening in the football field is immediately and unequivocally identified as a tackling. A *commonality with respect to interpretation* ('*eine Interpretationsgemeinschaft*', see Apel 1965, 1966) is thus tacitly and veridically assumed in every case.

This presupposed commonality is, of course, easily recognized in the case when the utterance 'Magnificent!' is triggered by what the two football fans have attended to right there and immediately before the intersubjectively established *here-and-now* of that utterance (see Figure 1): *what* is considered magnificent can under such conditions be made unequivocally known to the listener if and only if his strategy of segmentation and categorization of what happens in the field conforms to that of the speaker. The object of praise will for that reason remain only vaguely and partially known to a listener who happens to be a novice at the art of watching football games. Such a novice may, for instance, single out as the object of praise only the final sequences within the entire tackling manoeuvre. Within that restricted sequence, moreover, he may focus primarily upon, for example, speed of movement exhibited by the player rather than particular tactics by which his opponents are deceived.

The '*That*' of utterance (IV B) may hence—even under conditions of joint immediate or retroactive attendance to the same composite event—introduce *a state of intersubjectivity short of perfection, yet not so deficient that nothing can be made known*. The epistemological issue concerning what is 'really' praised by the football fan must consequently, when encountered within the actual context of human communication and the complete spatial–temporal–interpersonal framework of a particular act of speech, be translated into a question concerning potential and actually shared social realities. What is said about a particular tackling manoeuvre to a person who is not familiar with the rules of the football game resembles in some important respect what is said about President de Gaulle to an African who is not familiar with the game of modern French political life: what is made known is in both cases upon states of only partial intersubjectivity.

We have already indicated how retrospective attendance to the very same tackling manoeuvre under certain conditions may be established in a dialogue between two football fans after the game. Imagine, now, a case when retroactive attendance appears to be induced and confirmed by a similar exchange of utterances, but this time in a dialogue between an expert on football and a friend of his who knows only a little about the rules and the objectives of the game. Which message—if any at all—is under these conditions conveyed by an utterance such as 'That was magnificent!'? What, for instance, can be made known by the expert to the novice by the word 'That' on such an occasion?

In order to assess the impact of different categorizations upon subsequent, verbally induced identifying reference, we may possibly again resort to the film of the game. This time, however, rather subtle tests seem to be required. Both the speaker and the listener may, for instance, be asked to indicate, as precisely as possible, that 'That' of the utterance in terms of extension in real time. Partial commonality with respect to segmentation will then be reflected in largely, though not completely, overlapping sequences of the film. Additional discrimination tasks, moreover, may reveal that some attributes of the feat can be identified only by the expert, whereas others are easily recognized by the novice as well.

Such elaborate tests, however, can at best only serve to corroborate what we may infer on purely logical grounds: *what can be experientially established only as a partially shared social reality will remain only partially shared whenever that social reality is made the topic of a dialogue.* States of partial intersubjectivity due to divergent strategies of categorization are thus bound to be a recurrent theme in analysis of everyday—and even of scientific—human discourse, i.e. it will be the rule rather than the exception. If we conceive of the message as that which is made known, moreover, assessing message structure implies examining how what is said is nested on to only partially shared social realities in such a way that the realm of partially shared knowledge of a multifaceted social world on the part of the speaker and the listener is expanded and/or modified.

It is perfectly true that what is made known by the 'That' said by the football expert to the novice about a particular tackling falls short of perfect identifying reference as formally defined. It is equally true that the 'He' at an initial stage of the dialogue about President de Gaulle between the teacher of history and his African student is nested on to the latter's pre-established world only in very fragile ways. We have in both cases to do with acts of human communication that—when judged by criteria borrowed from the propositional calculus—neither appear to conform to the ideal of perfect 'Archimedean' convergence of identifying reference nor to fall into the abyss of the truth value gap. This state of mismatch between formal logic and instances of actual human discourse should not make us despair, however: the novice on football may himself one day become an expert, and the African student may some day know as much as—and even more than—his teacher about de Gaulle. The *states of only partial intersubjectivity*, the *openness of language towards experientially established social realities* and *its inherent potentialities of increased intersubjectivity in terms of contracts concerning shared strategies of categorization—these are indeed some of the outstanding aspects of natural language in action.* What appear as symptoms of imperfection and noise when some utterance is put into an externally provided straightjacket of propositional form and content thus become the pivot of theoretical inquiries when we seriously try to find out what is made known by that very utterance as an act of speech. Message structure must then be explored within the conceptual framework of the spatial–temporal interpersonal coordinates of that act of speech: whatever is made known is made known by an I to a you whose different, though partially shared, social worlds are temporarily brought into some state of intersection by virtue of the intersubjectively established *here-and-now* of their dialogue.

Let us now, with the aid of the conceptual skeleton of intersubjectivity portrayed in Figure 1, page 36, explore some universally recognized devices by which experientially established social realities—fully or partially shared or more or less veridically and reciprocally presupposed—may enter the act of speech. These are, first of all, the purely *deictic* segments of speech, also labelled 'shifters' and (in a philosophical discourse) 'indicators' or 'indexical signs': purely deictic segments are English words such as THIS / THAT; HERE / THERE; BEFORE / NOW / AFTERWARDS; I / YOU / THEY; and suffixes of verbs indicating tense. The point of reference for such segments is he temporarily established *here-and-now* of Figure 1, What is reciprocally assumed to constitute the focus of convergent attention or intention of the I and you may at that moment enter their dialogue as a THIS, HERE. What was attended to and/or talked about some time ago as well as what by both participants is cognized as located at a distance from their intersubjectively established here, on the other hand, may enter the act of speech as an intersubjectively established THAT, THERE.

I have elsewhere (Rommetveit 1968a, pp. 46–54 and 190–7, 1972a, pp. 218–40, 1972c, pp. 45–52) tried to explore deixis as explicated in linguistic analysis, in the light of psychological inquiries into the social interaction and self–other relationships involved, and from the point of view of a hermeneutic philosophy of language. The term '*deixis*' stems from the Greek word for showing, pointing out. Deictic elements may be said to point out experientially available, talked-about and to-be-talked-about social realities by tagging them on to the spatial–temporal–interpersonal coordinates of the act of speech. All natural languages contain deictic devices, and Weinreich comments upon such devices as follows.

(Weinreich 1963, p. 123) Among the factors of the speech situation which are utilized in deixis are the following: the utterer of the discourse ('1st person') or the receiver ('2nd person'); the time of discourse (tense) and its place (varieties of demonstration); and the identity or non-identity of the act of discourse (anaphora, reflexiveness, obviation, etc.). That this paradigm constitutes a striking universal of language can be appreciated not only from its wide-spread distribution, but also by visualizing further factors of the speech situation which could be, but do not seem to be, utilized in any language . . . .

Deictic devices—while of only peripheral concern to linguists assessing syntactic structures and 'readings' of sentences *in vacuo*—have remained a topic of central interest to linguists who, like Wittgenstein in his *Philosophical Investigations*, clearly realized that what is made known can only be assessed by a careful analysis of the intricate relationships between what is said and extralinguistic features of the act of speech. Thus Uhlenbeck, commenting upon the neglect of such relationships in the early days of the Harvard–M.I.T. school, wrote:

> (Uhlenbeck 1963, p. 11) Every sentence needs to be interpreted in the light of various extra-linguistic data. These data are (1) the situation in which the sentence is spoken, (2) the preceding sentences, if any, (3) the hearer's knowledge of the speaker and the topics which might be discussed with him . . . .

We have already shown how some initially experientially established social reality may be retroactively attended to as the referent of 'That' of a particular act of speech via preceding definite expressions such as 'the slim, funny-looking quarterback . . .' and 'the manoeuvre . . .' (see p. 30). Reichling (1963) aptly describes the general linguistic function of such definite descriptions as '*an as-knowndeclaration*' ('*eine Als-bekannt-Setzung*'). What is described is thus *not* made publicly known, but only assumed (by the speaker) to be known already by both participants in the dialogue by virtue of shared experiences and/or pre-established intersections of their social worlds. And it will serve to establish convergent identifying reference if and only if the speaker's assumption concerning intersection of pre-established social worlds is correct. A proper name, for instance, will under most conditions fail as a foundation for partial intersubjectivity unless both the speaker and the listener already know that person by name.

The openness of the act of speech towards experientially established social realities is at a maximum for segments of utterances such as THIS and THAT. THIS may refer to whatever is jointly attended to at the moment it has been uttered, be it an ashtray in front of the listener and the speaker or some philosophical issue in which they are jointly immersed. THAT serves to bring into their dialogue whatever is veridically assumed to be identified by both of them at some distance from the origo of intersubjectivity at that instant, i.e. as further away from the momentary *here-and-now* of the act of speech.

Pronouns such as HE, SHE and IT, on the other hand, being only partially open, involve contracts with respect to widely shared modes of categorization as well. The peronal pronoun HE, for instance, serves to single out one presumedly already (or to-be-) identified male person who is neither engaged as an I nor as a you in that particular act of speech. And subtle combinations of deictic and designative functions are in some languages involved in pronouns of address. The you of the act of speech is thus in German addressed as either 'Sie' or 'du', in French as either 'vous' or 'tu'. Thus, person deixis does not only involve universally shared modes of categorization such as identification of sex, but may even mirror subtle experientially founded and institutionalized social realities of stratification, power and solidarity (Brown and Gilman 1966). A sudden switch from 'tu' to 'vous' in a dialogue between two French-speaking persons may actually signal intentionally increased distance—and even alienation—from the person who until that moment has been addressed as 'tu'. Alternative forms of address thus represent options with respect to self–other relationships involved in acts of speech.

These are rather subtle aspects of deixis, however, whose ontogenetic basis has been explored by Piaget penetrating inquiries into *egocentrism* and *decentration*. The egocentric child appears to engage in communication on the tacit assumption that the world is unequivocal and monistic: his immediate *here-and-now* constitutes the centre of whatever world he can share with others. An object at the centre of his visual field may hence be talked about *as if* it were equally visible to and immediately identified by the person he is talking to as well, even in cases when it is in fact invisible to the latter. A state of egocentricity may therefore be described as a collapse of the *I–you coordinate* in Figure 1, page 36. Ontogenetically, a stage of egocentrism represents in a way the initial imprisonment in the immediate *here-and-now*, i.e. an initial and unreflected diffusion of perspectives which at some later stage are spontaneously mastered as the point of view of *the I versus* that of *the you*.

A characteristic feature of the egocentric stage is thus an incapacity to adopt the perspective of the other person and such failures were frequently noticed by Piaget in his early studies of children's speech (Piaget 1926). A six-year-old child telling a fairy tale to another child who has never heard that tale before may, for instance, suddenly introduce some 'he' or 'she' who has not been mentioned at all *as if* that person were already familiar to the listener. His narrative may thus run as follows: 'There was once a king, and there was a prince. And that dragon. And the dragon was very angry, and he wanted to kill her' . . . . 'Her' is in such a case referring to a *princess* who at that moment happens to be at the centre of the speaker's world of imagination and, *eo ipso*, is tacitly assumed to be immediately identified by his listener as well.

The capacity for decentration may be explored in fairly simple experimental contexts in which some object takes on different shapes depending upon the location from which it is being viewed. The child is given ample opportunity to view the object from, for example, location X as well as from location Y. Emancipation from imprisonment in his immediate *here-and-now* is inferred if he can conceive of the shape of the object as viewed from point X while actually viewing it from point Y. Studies of decentration, however, also encompass experiments in which the child is requested to sort or order multidimensional objects. His capacity for decentration is under such conditions revealed in performances requiring cross-classification and simultaneous attendance to multiple attributes (Smedslund 1964).

Decentration as conceived of by Piaget is thus a very general and composite developmental process by which an individual acquires the capacity to adopt a variety of interrelated perspectives and strategies of categorization in response to successively more highly differentiated multifaceted objects, events and states of affairs. States of intersubjectivity established at particular stages of specific dialogues may consequently, as indicated earlier, be explored in terms of potentially shared perspectives and the capacity of one participant to adopt the point of view of the other. These are distinctive features of the dialogue as a social activity, as characteristic of the nearly perfectly established intersubjectivity in the case of the brooding couple of the fragile connections between two very different social worlds in the case of the teacher of French history and his African student at an early stage of their dialogue.

The openness of language towards intuitively and experientially established shared knowledge and the embeddedness of the act of speech in social life are central and recurrent themes in *hermeneutic philosophy of language*. We have already indicated how less than perfect convergence with respect to segmentation and categorization of composite events makes for only partially shared social realities. We have shown, moreover, how what is experientially only partially shared reappears as only partially shared when introduced by a deictic THAT. Purely deictic words may hence, according to some hermeneutic philosophers of language, be conceived of as channels by which largely experientially established, intuitive and only partially shared knowledge invades the domain of verbal communication. Apel, referring to Wittgenstein's reflections on language games, writes:

> (Apel 1966, p. 72) ... the 'deep grammar' of the sentence modes cannot be restricted to those *typical* forms which are usually differentiated in traditional grammar. Such a restriction is invalid, since it is contradicted by the fact that a sentence is initially endowed with meaning because it is placed in the context of a wider meaning which is composed of language and the practice of living, i.e. precisely in the context of the 'language game'.
> (Apel 1968, p. 39) In order to achieve a constitution of meaning the mind must be fully engaged; that is, it must be *genuinely engaged in the here and now*. Every constitution of meaning refers back to *an individual perspective, to a standpoint, or in other words to a bodily engagement (Leibengagement) of the cognizing mind.*
> (Italics mine)

We shall return to some of the central themes of hermeneutic philosophy of language in Chapter V. What is said about 'bodily engagement' (*Leibengagement*) and the mind being 'genuinely engaged in the here and now' by Apel as well as by Habermas (1968), however, seems to be at variance with Piaget's analysis of prerequisities for mastery of deixis. *The capacity for decentration is in fact, as already indicated, a capacity to transcend the egocentric here-and-now by temporarily adopting the perspective of the other person.* What is made known during a dialogue cannot hence be accounted for in terms of an interaction between two people, each of whom is imprisoned in a *here-and-now* as defined by his own individual bodily engagement, interest and intention. And Wittgenstein's metaphor about language games must clearly be interpreted in the light of his reflections concerning the futility of making known so-called purely 'private experiences' (Wittgenstein 1968).

Deictic words are in view of these reflections, as well as in view of the capacity for decentration involved in mastery of deixis, not merely openings towards intuitive, experientially established knowledge of a '*Lebenswelt*', but also foundations upon which increasingly intersubjective and even 'public' knowledge can be established: what can be *made known* is by definition restricted to what can be *shared* in some sense. Increasing capacity to single out abstract and distinctive aspects or features of objects and events implies increasing capacity for emancipation from immediate 'bodily engagement' in those objects and events—and hence also increasing capacity for communication about them.

This has already been indicated in our earlier discussion of metaphors and of linguistically provided options with respect to a range of alternative perspectives. Thus, your impression of a particular person you know may have the status of purely 'private experience' until the moment when somebody asks you how he is. What you on that occasion make known by your answer, however, is no longer merely private experience. The very word 'communication' stems from the Latin verb *communicare, to make common or shared*. And what is made known to your listener by either 'He has the capacity to gain pleasure from small things' or 'He is easy to please' is in fact contingent upon shared cognitive capacities such as (a) attributing easiness and difficulty to tasks and (b) decentered shifts of perspectives with respect to persons. Decentration and the capacity of one participant in the dialogue to adopt a perspective proposed by the other participant are thus required in order to establish some shared perspective on what until then remained private experience. And you have the option of employing either one of the two expressions cited above if and only if both your listener and you master abstract strategies of categorization by virtue of which persons can be considered possessors of talents as well as (aspects of) tasks.

Purely deictic words such as THIS and THAT are also labelled 'shifters': what at any particular moment of a dialogue is singled out as an object of joint attention by such word shifts in accordance with changing extralinguistic conditions and with what at that particular moment happens to constitute the intersubjectively established *here-and-now*. A mixed deictic–designative word such as the personal pronoun HE, moreover, serves on different occasions to establish convergent attendance towards different male persons, depending upon, for example, which one of them is being pointed at by the speaker at that moment or which one of them was talked about a moment ago. This openness, however, pertains not only to deictic words, but also to definite expressions such as, for example, THE MAN or THE ROCK. What is reciprocally (by speaker and listener) identified by means of such expressions can therefore only be assessed by examining what is assumed as already known.

This implies, among other things, that very little can be inferred concerning 'literal' and 'metaphorical readings' of sentences *as such*, under conditions of ignorance with respect to the intersubjectively established *here-and-now* of the act of speech. Consider, for example, the following sentence:

(IV F) The rock is becoming brittle with age.

The sentence is borrowed from Michael Reddy, who comments upon it as follows:

(Reddy 1969, p. 242) . . . consider the readings assigned to (IV F) in the context of (1) a group of people on a geology expedition and (2) a group of students walking out of the office of some staunch old professor emeritus. . . . In context (1), (IV F) will almost certainly function literally. In context (2), however, one can say with equal certainty that *part* of (IV F)—namely '*rock*' and '*brittle*'—will function metaphorically, while the rest remains perfectly literal.

Reddy may be perfectly correct on his conclusions, but he fails to specify precisely how and by which features of the acts of communication the externally described contexts are supposed to affect what is being made known. We may perhaps contribute towards a further explication of these issues by visualizing a third extralinguistic frame: the staunch old professor may himself be a geologist who has joined the expedition, and he may during the act of speech even be viewed by the speaker as standing in front of the rock. What will be singled out as the referent of '*The rock*' in (IV F) can clearly in such a case *not* be assessed without examining which *here-and-now* has been established by the speaker and the listener at the moment (IV F) is being said. We may even imagine a situation in which 'literal' *and* 'metaphorical' functions are served by the very same utterance. Two students may, for instance, both be viewing the professor emeritus as he is posing against the background of a brittle rock. Assuming such convergence with respect to gaze as well as with respect to perceptual organization of what is attended to at that moment, one of them may say to the other 'The rocks are both becoming brittle with age'.

The mere physical presence of rocks or old professors in the geographical vicinity of the location at which the act of speech takes place is thus as such of hardly any significance at all as far as interpretation of (IV F) is concerned. Moreover, a public inventory of persons, objects and features of the landscape, even if possible, will serve hardly any purpose. The linguistically relevant extralinguistic context enters the dialogue only as cognized by the participants. It must hence be explored as that which is already attended to and/or potentially shared within a temporarily established framework such as the one suggested in Figure 1, page 36. In other words, *the extralinguistic context cannot be assessed 'publicly' or 'privately', but only in terms of the architecture of intersubjectivity at the moment of speech*.

Some of the significant implications of this approach may hopefully become more visible against the background of the expanded Harvard–M.I.T. semantics of (contextual) presuppositions and 'readings' of sentences (see pp. 15). Let us therefore examine how Chomsky in his recent work deals with one specific case in which extralinguistic conditions are brought to bear upon the interpretation of what is said. Consider the following sentence:

(IV G) I am not against MY FATHER, only against THE LABOR MINISTER.

Chomsky comments upon this sentence as follows:

(Chomsky 1972, p. 67) *Knowing* ... that the speaker is the son of the labor minister, *we* would assign to this utterance a reading in which *the emphasized phrases are coreferential*. On one reading *the sentence is contradictory*, but knowing the facts just cited[3] a more natural interpretation would be that the speaker is opposed to what his father does in his capacity as labor minister, and would be accurately paraphrased in this more elaborate way. It is hardly obvious that what we 'read into' sentences in such ways as these—no doubt, in a fairly systematic way—can either be sharply dissociated from grammatically determined readings, on the one hand, or from considerations of fact and belief, on the other. (Italics mine)

This passage may serve as a point of departure for explicating the notions of coreference (and hence of identifying reference) in the expanded Harvard–M.I.T. approach. Notice, first of all, how coreference is dealt with by Chomsky: '*Knowing* ... that the speaker is the son of the labor minister, *we* would assign ... a reading ...'. The inference from extralinguistic 'facts' to 'readings' is thus apparently based upon an assessment of presuppositions which is 'public' in some sense. But who are the knowing and reading–assigning '*we*' in this case? If they are the linguists or the hearers, which tacit assumptions are made with respect to socially shared knowledge? What difference does it make, for instance, whether the speaker is assumed to know that they know?

Chomsky finds, on at least one reading, (IV G) contradictory: assuming that MY FATHER and THE LABOR MINISTER refer to the same person X, (IV G) can be read as depicting a state of being not against X and being against X. Such a state is known as a state of ambivalence. When temporarily accepting Chomsky's insistence on a two-valued logic, we have thus to apologize to psychiatrists and clinical psychologists: what is rejected when gauged against criteria borrowed from the propositional calculus may indeed in a dialogue between a patient and his therapist be attended to as particularly significant segments of discourse.

Adhering to Chomsky's criteria for assessing coreference and contradiction, however, reason and plausibility can be restored if we paraphrase (IV G) as follows:

(IV G') I am not against MY FATHER only against WHAT MY FATHER DOES IN HIS CAPACITY AS LABOR MINISTER.

Imagine, however, a situation in which the speaker is engaged in a dialogue with a friend. Knowing, of course, that his friend knows he is the son of the labor minister, he says:

(a) 'I am strongly opposed to the way our government is organized. The insulation of labor affairs into a separate ministry, detached from the ministry for industrial development, is silly. I have nothing against what my father does in his capacity as labor minister. Hardly any other person could do better. *I am not against MY FATHER, only against THE LABOR MINISTER.*'

(IV G) may thus in this context be paraphrased as, for example:

(IV G") I am not against MY FATHER, only against THE LABOR MINISTER AS A GOVERNMENTAL POSITION.

Consider, next, a dialogue in which (IV G) is uttered by a speaker who is not related to the labor minister at all as far as he himself knows. The dialogue runs as follows:

(b) 'I don't like the labor minister.'

'Oh, you don't like him. Are you repelled by his mixture of benevolence and authoritarianism, by his paternal appearance?'

'No, you are wrong. I don't mind his posing as a father figure at all. My being against him has nothing to do with that. I am solely concerned with his policy, with the decisions he makes in his capacity as a labor minister. *I am not against MY FATHER, only against THE LABOR MINISTER.*'

The last utterance may thus be paraphrased as, for example:

(IV G''') *I am not against MY FATHER, only against WHAT THE LABOR MINISTER DOES IN HIS CAPACITY AS LABOR MINISTER.*

The first and fundamental lesson to be learned from these examples is very simple: 'facts' concerning coreference, i.e. whether the speaker actually is the son of the labor minister or not, have *as such* no bearing whatsoever upon 'readings' of the expressions MY FATHER and THE LABOR MINISTER. Thus, the speaker may in case (b) in fact be the illegitimate son of the labor minister. The fact may even be publicly documented, we (the linguists) may know it, and the listener may know it as well. It will be of no relevance at all with respect to what is made known by (IV G), however, unless the speaker knows it and knows that his listener knows as well.

Consider, next, only situations in which the latter condition of intersubjectivity is fulfilled, i.e. what is made known by (IV G) when the fact of coreference has been established as a shared social reality at the moment of the act of speech. How, precisely, does such a state of affairs affect the 'reading' of the expression THE LABOR MINISTER?

Chomsky indicates one possible 'reading' in paraphrase (IV G'): the speaker may under such conditions make known that he is only against WHAT the person he is talking about DOES IN HIS CAPACITY AS LABOR MINISTER. As shown in case (b), however, such a reading is equally possible and plausible in a situation in which both the speaker and the listener know that the former is *not* the son of the labor minister. And an entirely different 'reading' seems in fact required under conditions of intersubjectively established coreference such as those indicated in case (a).

Chomsky's inference from 'facts' of coreference to 'readings' of (IV G) thus appears to be of an *ad hoc* nature, and the second and far more difficult lesson to be learned from it can only be learned if we venture to examine which tacit assumptions may be involved. What notion of identifying reference must be endorsed as a point of departure for his inference? *What, precisely, is the 'reading' of (IV G) on which 'the sentence is contradictory'?*

In order to pursue this issue, we shall have to extrapolate from Chomsky's analysis of (IV G) to relatively simple, but similar sentences. Being a Scandinavian, I may for instance be asked by a friend from the U.S.A. *'Do you know Ingmar Bergman?'* My honest answer is such a situation will be:

(IV H) I know THE ARTIST, but not THE PERSON.

A similar dialogue may occur if I happen to live next to our labor minister. Knowing that, one of my colleagues may during our conversation at lunch say

48

to me 'You have the labor minister as your next door neighbour, I have heard. How is he?'. And my answer on such an occasion may be:

(IV K) *I like THE NEIGHBOUR, but not THE POLITICIAN.*

And such answers may be compared to very ordinary quests for information at the very beginning of some dialogue such as:

(IV L) *Do you know THE LABOR MINISTER?*

Extrapolating from Chomsky's re-'reading' of (IV G) based upon 'fact' of coreference, we are forced to conclude that some other entity is being referred to by THE LABOR MINISTER under such conditions than, for example, the entity referred to by the same expression in (IV L). Moreover, sentences such as (IV H) and (IV K) must according to his criteria in some readings be contradictory. Thus, either THE ARTIST or THE PERSON or both expressions should be 'read' in a different way under the condition of intersubjectively established coreference of (IV H) as compared to a condition otherwise similar except for the fact of coreference. Following Chomsky, therefore, *one* or *the other* or *both* of the emphasized phrases in (IV H) must be 'read' in a way different from what would be the case if I, being asked whether I know Ingmar Bergman, answered *either*:

(IV M) I know THE ARTIST,

or:

(IV N) I do not know THE PERSON.

It is only when pushed into such a queer position that the 'underlying' or 'deep' notion of identifying reference of the expanded Harvard–M.I.T. approach can be smoked out of its *ad hoc* holes of apparent plausibility. And what emerges from those holes is in fact the familiar, scholastic and 'Archimedean' notion, i.e. the notion of identifying reference as an unequivocally defined point in a monistic and epistemological transparent space, constructed on axiomatic prerequisites for specific operations within formal logic. A definite expression must be conceived of as corresponding to one and only one such point in order to enter the realm in which unequivocal truth values can be computed. And two definite expressions are by definition coreferential if and only if projected on to the same point.

The person talked about in (IV M) and (IV N) is hence—even though he happens to be Ingmar Bergman—not allowed at all to enter the dialogue as a multifaceted and only partially known entity: the severe laws of the truth values prescribe that the speaker must know him fully or not at all. Conditions of partial knowledge of persons and recognition of a given person as a composite and multifacted social reality must *eo ipso* be dealt with by semanticists of the Harvard–M.I.T. school only in exceptional cases such as (IV G), (IV H) and (IV K). The general formula for re-'reading' of coreferential definite expressions in such cases must consequently serve as a device by which in principle indivisible entities each can be split up into equally indivisible parts.

What initially—from our entirely different approach to the dialogue—appeared as formalistic escapism appears upon a closer examination to constitute a logical dilemma as well. Consider, for instance, the following dialogue:

'Do you know Ingmar Bergman?'

'Yes.' (1)

'Do you know him well?'

'Well, I certainly know him as an artist. Do you want to test me? I am sure I shall be able to single out any previously unknown movie made by him from a sample of other movies you would consider very similar.' (2)

'Do you know him personally? Have you ever met him?'

'No, I don't know the person.' (3)

The Chomskian dilemma is encountered the moment we try to transcribe such a dialogue into propositional language with the objective of capturing what is sequentially made known. We may try to transcribe what I 'assert' at stages (1), (2) and (3) as follows:[4]

(p) I know X.

(q) I know X' as Y.

(r) I don't know X" as Z.

Notice, first of all, the contradiction between assigning an unequivocal truth value at stage (1) and the assumption—clearly endorsed by the interrogator—that something can be added to what has been made known at that stage. Obviously, (p) cannot be considered as either unequivocally true or unequivocally false unless X has been unequivocally identified. In that case, however, *nothing more can be made known* about (my knowledge of) X at all.

Suppose, however, that this dilemma were solved in some way. Other problems would then immediately be encountered, and this time especially in our attempts at capturing the interrelationships between what presumedly is asserted at successive stages of the conversation. How, for instance, is it possible to cope with the issue of coreference across (p), (q) and (r) in such a way that all three of them can enter the same composite propositional expression? In what sense can X, X' and X" be considered coreferential? Or, in less technical terms: *assuming that Ingmar Bergman constitutes the sustained topic of the dialogue, in what sense does that topic remain 'the same' at stage (3) as at stage (1)?*

These are issues we have already dealt with at some length, and we have tried to show how they can be transformed into intuitively plausible and even empirically feasible inquiries within our alternative conceptual framework. My 'Yes' at stage (1) of the dialogue is thus, when viewed from the point of view of the architecture of intersubjectivity, merely an initial and fragile connection between two social worlds. Utterances of the form 'I know X', in which 'X' is a proper name are thus informative, yet in themselves entirely undetermined when gauged against criteria from the propositional calculus (see Stalnaker 1972, p. 385). They remain undetermined and entirely open with respect to which aspect(s) of X I claim to know.

What is left undetermined by the proper name, however, may become partially determined by such expressions as 'in his capacity as labor minister', 'as an artist', 'the person', 'the neighbour', 'the politician', etc. Each such expression serves to specify some presumedly shared perspective or strategy of categorization that may be jointly adopted by the two participants in the dialogue. And specification may in turn make it possible even to verify what has been asserted. The speaker's claim that he knows Ingmar Bergman THE ARTIST may be tested by procedures proposed by himself at stage (2) of the dialogue. His claim that he does not know Ingmar Bergman THE PERSON may be corroborated by the observation that he cannot identify Bergman when the latter is viewed on a picture together with many other male persons.

The capacity to adopt different perspectives testifies to decentered shifts of categorization: other human beings are at least as multifaceted as the role relationships by virtue of which they are engaged in social life and interpersonal relations, and they may hence be known and talked about from a variety of different points of view. Switching from one potential perspective to another may on some occasions resemble the switch from one to the other of two distinctively different perceptual organizations of the same visual display. My *liking THE NEIGHBOUR* while *not liking THE POLITICIAN* is thus, in a sense, analogous to my finding the young lady attractive and the 'mother-in-law' rather ugly in Figure 2. And coreference is in principle equally irrelevant in the two cases: as applied to cognition of other human beings, full mastery of decentration implies in fact that I can view a man in his capacity as a politician independently of how he appears to me as a neighbour. Assuming such different potential perspectives *and* mastery of decentration, there is thus no contradiction at all inherent in what is made known by sentences such as (IV G), (IV H) and (IV K) under conditions of so-called 'coreference'.

Leeper's ambiguous figure may thus serve as a point of departure for further explications of openness and partial determination encountered at various

FIGURE 2. Leeper's 'wife and mother-in-law'. From Leeper, J. Genet. Psychol., **46**, 41–75

stages of a dialogue. We have already shown how a 'That' said about a feat in a football field and a 'he' said about President de Gaulle may refer to only partially shared social realities. Other variants of openness and partial determination are encountered when a deictic 'he', even though tagged on to a proper name, leaves entirely open which aspect(s) of 'him' is being talked about. The presupposed sustained topic may in one case be 'he' in his capacity as a football player, in another case 'he' as an artist. What is presupposed in such a case, however, may perhaps within our conceptual framework of intersubjectivity most appropriately be conceived of as established by means of tacitly endorsed contracts with respect to categorization.

IV. 2. Complementarity, Contracts and Language Games

We have already briefly commented upon the recent expansion of scope within the Harvard–M.I.T. school of linguistics: the 'propositional content' of a sentence is no longer to be identified *in vacuo*, but has to be assessed against the contextual background of what is being presupposed. In order to find out what is asserted when something is said, the linguist is thus obliged to examine what is already assumed to be the case at the moment of speech. He must consequently, like the student of literature, try to assess what is made known by a fragment of a text against the background of the more inclusive discourse of which that fragment constitutes an integral part.

As shown in the preceding chapter, moreover, the linguistically relevant 'reality' at any particular stage of a dialogue is by definition the intersubjectively established reality *here-and-now* at that stage of communication. Extralinguistic 'facts', common beliefs and widely shared presuppositions are therefore as such—however veridically and publicly assessed—of no immediate significance. They can enter the dialogue and affect what is made known only through the participants, i.e. *qua* features of their temporarily and partially shared social world. And the same holds true for communication between a creative writer and his reader: what is made known to the reader the moment he is reading one particular passage of a novel is only intelligible within the framework of a shared imaginary world and the intersubjectively established *here-and-now* of that particular passage.

The relationship between such intersubjectively established worlds of imagination and 'ordinary reality' constitutes a recurrent issue in literary analysis. Thus, Wellek maintains:

(Wellek 1966, pp. 410–11) The world of objects which poetry and fiction build up in our imagination is of course not identical with that of ordinary reality. It is related to reality. For instance, we could describe the world of Dickens, postillions, old inns, fog, etc. or that of Dostoevsky, the dusty slums of Petersburg, the dreary provincial towns, easily enough; but there are other worlds more difficult to describe, like those of Valery or Rilke. These worlds are obviously selective, even idiosyncratic, and they may be quite fantastic structures, distortions of reality like Kafka's world. But still the world of the poet is related to ordinary reality, and we cannot, in literary criticism, escape the issue of this relationship to reality.

What, then, can be meant by 'ordinary reality' in connection with fiction and poetry? And how, more precisely, does reading of fiction differ from, for example, reading about previously unknown, but real, historical events?

We have in preceding chapters indicated how *purely 'private' experience is transformed into intersubjectively established knowledge by the very act of communication.* The speaker's 'experiential reality' will in such a case never be made known to the listener as such, in its initial pre-verbal richness and complexity. Which aspects can be made known are partly dependent upon pre-established commonality between the two participants in the dialogue with respect to interpretation, strategies of attribution and cognitive categorization. And such pre-established commonality appears to be a prerequisite for communication, regardless of whether the topic constitutes fiction or fact.

The world of the creative writer is clearly related to 'ordinary reality' in the sense that it is accessible to the reader by virtue of his mastery of ordinary language only. It is certainly selective, but so also are written reports on real events and states of affairs. Kuhn (1970, p. 164) maintains that even the most esoteric poet is far more concerned than the scientist with lay approbation of his creative work. And lay approbation implies—at least on some occasions—a confirmation that intersubjectivity has been established.

So far, we have tried to examine the architecture of intersubjectivity primarily as it is revealed under conditions of normal, everyday, face-to-face communication. What emerges from our preceding analysis of the dialogue and the temporarily shared social world is, first of all, only a skeleton of intersubjectivity in the form of the spatial–temporal–interpersonal coordinates of the act of speech. Such a skeleton becomes the framework of a partially shared social world, however, only by virtue of some pre-established commonality with respect to interpretation, to the extent that the participants in the act of communication are capable of decentered shifts of perspectives, and as a result of temporary convergence with respect to categorization of multifaceted objects, events and states of affairs.

These features appear to remain remarkably invariant across fiction and fact as well as across oral and written communication, and they appear indeed to be prerequisites for successful human communication. *The social psychological foundation of intersubjectivity, however, can hardly be fully understood unless we also explore what happens when that foundation appears to break down.* Let us at this stage therefore make a brief excursion to studies of basic communication disorders.

Perhaps the most intriguing, but at the same time most revealing, cases of communication breakdown are encountered in studies of schizophrenic language and thought. Gregory Bateson and his coworkers have been particularly concerned with the ontogenesis of autism and schizophrenia, and especially with the matrix of interpersonal relations out of which such pathologies develop (see Bateson *et al.* 1956, Watzlawick *et al.* 1967). And the image of the early social world of the schizophrenic which emerges out of their studies is an image of a chaotic world, replete with ambivalent attitudes and internally contradictory I–you relationships.

The ambivalence of the powerful 'significant other' towards the highly dependent child is revealed in characteristic recurrent patterns of interaction coined '*double binds*'. The essence of a double bind is the communication of contradictory and mutually exclusive, though concomitant, messages. The mother may for instance signal an invitation for contact and approach by extending her arms towards the child, while at the same time rejection and avoidance are being conveyed by her concomitant frozen smile and the harsh, metallic flavour of her voice. The child is hence imprisoned in a dilemma from which there is no opportunity to escape. Whatever he does—whether he approaches the extended arms or withdraws from the hostile facial expression—he is bound to behave contrary to premises and expectations on the part of 'the significant other'. The child's assumptions concerning what is presupposed by the adult will under such conditions again and again be disconfirmed.

The schizophrenic's characteristic withdrawal from 'ordinary reality' is, when viewed in such an ontogenetic perspective, a withdrawal from any kind of temporarily shared social reality. The basic prerequisites for normal human communication seem to have collapsed. His grasp of reality fails in the sense that he has no faith whatsoever that other people share his perspective on states of affairs, and he does not know what is 'real' any longer because the very foundation of intersubjectivity seems to have broken down. His behaviour appears therefore bizarre and incomprehensible to others, and what he says often does not make sense at all. A closer examination of his symptoms, however, reveals considerable internal coherence. And the characteristic internal coherence behind his apparent incoherence provides us with clues to features of verbal communication so basic as to be hardly ever noticed at all under conditions of normal discourse.

One such characteristic symptom is the so-called homonym symptom. The schizophrenic patient may, for instance, start out telling about a grand celebration, and he says:

(IV O) I too was invited, I went to the ball ... and it rolled and rolled away ...

His intention is in this case clearly to make known something about the ball to which he was invited and what happened at that ball. While listening, we immediately comprehend what is said because we are spontaneously decoding it in accordance with the speaker's intention and *on his, the speaker's premises*. Our anticipations are intuitively monitored in accordance with *his* narrative. We are, therefore, as listeners, engaged in the *here-and-now* of the act of speech, at each successive stage of the narrative immediately intelligible in terms of what the speaker already has made known to us and assumes to know. At the moment of his pause, we thus very likely expect him to continue with 'and then ...' or some such expression. We know he has been invited to that ball, he is going there, and we expect him to make known what happens next.

It is precisely at this moment, however, that our firmly rooted, though entirely intuitive and unreflective, assumption concerning complementarity between the act of speaking and that of listening is disconfirmed. Having uttered 'the ball . . .', the schizophrenic seems to stumble, in a way. His act of speech is disrupted, his story does not continue in accordance with what he initially intended to make known. He pauses, apparently bewildered by what he himself has just uttered. Trying to make sense of one particular segment of his own speech *in vacuo*, entirely detached from the unequivocal context which constitutes part of our shared social world at that very moment, he is genuinely confused. What has been conveyed by the homonymous expression? *What can be made known by such an ambiguous segment of discourse to people who may not share his social world at all?*

His answer represents a perfectly rational solution to this riddle once we endorse *his* basic distrust in intersubjectivity and accept the riddle as such. The spoken form 'ball' is, of course, also the word for very familiar objects: it refers to toys of a spherical shape, used for play and in a variety of athletic games. And it is in fact far more frequently used in discourse about such objects than in the way the schizophrenic had intended to use it on this occasion. What he says after the pause about rolling is thus in some respect a 'publicly' plausible completion of his act of speech. Instead of finishing what he intended to say—assuming, in that case, that we have adopted a perspective induced by him and that we are listening on his premises—he simply tries to complete something he most likely may have said under conditions when no such complementarity between speaking and listening can be assumed.

As we try to explore the architecture of intersubjectivity in the light of such pathologies, we are forced to return once more to the interpersonal coordinate of the act of speech (see Figure 1, p. 36). What, more precisely, is tacitly and veridically assumed concerning complementarity between speaking and listening under normal conditions of human discourse? We began our explorations of the architecture of intersubjectivity by examining cases of human communication under conditions of interpersonally firmly established social realities and nearly perfect complementarity. Since then, we have tried to explore what kind of contracts are being spontaneously and reciprocally adhered to under such optimal conditions of communication, and we have attempted to examine what those contracts may imply by inquiring into cases when normal and habitually endorsed contracts of communication apparently are *not* fulfilled. Thus, capacity for decentration becomes an important feature of intersubjectivity in the light of Piaget's studies of egocentric thought and language: the tacitly and reciprocally assumed interpersonally established social world of the adult dialogue can only be fully understood when contrasted with the egocentric child's imprisonment in his private and immediate *here-and-now*.

Bateson and his coworkers, moreover, direct our attention to other aspects of intersubjectivity, and to violations of tacit contracts for communication due to anomalous interpersonal relations. Serious breakdowns of communication in cases of schizophrenia *cannot* be attributed to incapacity for decentration. What seems to be at stake is rather faith in social confirmation of experientially established reality and *sustained control of the immediate here-and-now*. The schizophrenic's situation is consequently characterized by alienation and incapacity to impose his own world upon others in such a way as to achieve intersubjectivity. The disruption of the act of speech revealed in the homonym symptom seems to testify to an oscillation between a private and a strangely 'public' frame of reference on the part of the speaker. His pause after having uttered '*the ball . . .*' signals loss of control, in a way: he seems to be listening to himself as if what is made known is something entirely detached from what he intended to say a moment ago.

Tacitly endorsed rules concerning temporary control of the *here-and-now* of the dialogue are, of course, part of the basic complementarity inherent in the I–you coordinate of any normal and intuitively performed act of speech (see Figure 1, p. 36). And control is spontaneously, by tacit and reciprocal presuppositions, unequivocally linked to direction of communication: *the speaking I has the privilege of pointing out the objects, events and states of affairs to enter the field of intersubjectively shared attention.* Which of all possible entities of an experientially shared situation will be introduced and enter the slots of THIS, HERE and THAT, THERE of the formal skeleton of intersubjectivity is thus at any phase of the act of speech in principle determined by the speaker. The same holds true for any topic, whether introduced by deixis, by identifying descriptions, or by other means. The listening you will hence, if tests of identifying reference are conducted, as a rule be asked to identify a target as defined by the speaker. Being the listener, he has to accept and engage in whatever social reality is being introduced into the formal framework of intersubjectivity the moment 'silence is transformed into speech'.

And this is exactly what *we* do when listening to a segment of a narrative such as (IV O): we assume as already known, and on the premises of the speaker, what *he* at each successive stage has introduced into the temporarily shared social world. As the schizophrenic is uttering 'the ball . . .', we thus spontaneously make sense of what he is saying in terms of the as-already-known ball to which he has been invited. Our decoding of the first part of his utterance is thus spontaneously geared towards what we assume he intends to make known, and it is based on the tacit assumption that the speaker is monitoring what he says in accordance with what he assumes to constitute our temporarily shared social world. The full-fledged act of verbal communication is thus under normal conditions based upon a reciprocally endorsed and spontaneously fulfilled contract of complementarity: *encoding* is tacitly assumed to involve *anticipatory decoding*, i.e. it is taken for granted that speech is continuously listener-oriented and monitored in accordance with assumptions concerning a *shared* social world and convergent strategies of categorization. Conversely—and on precisely those premises—*decoding* is tacitly assumed to be speaker-oriented and aiming at *a reconstruction of what the speaker intends to make known.*

The schizophrenic's stumbling in the homonym may thus most appropriately be conceived of as an impressive, although entirely misplaced, shift of cognitive perspective on what he himself has just said. Indeed, his 'reading' of the homonymous expression reveals a sensitivity to ambiguities and potential meanings nearly equal to that of the presumedly entirely decentered linguist when the latter is reflecting upon possible readings of an expression *in vacuo.* The schizophrenic, however, being actively engaged in an act of communication, has an immediate commitment to the intersubjectively established *here-and-now* of his own act of speech. His re-'reading' is thus in view of his role as a speaker a symptom of extreme alienation: it goes contrary to what we, his listeners in accordance with his own intention veridically have accepted as the temporarily shared social reality.

Intersubjectivity has thus to be taken for granted in order to be achieved. It is based on mutual faith in a shared social world, and decentration constitutes part of its foundation if and only if monitored in accordance with a reciprocally endorsed contract of complementarity. Our immediate interaction with others is constantly based on the tacit and firm assumption of some commonality with respect to interpretation (*'eine Interpretationsgemeinschaft'*). As listeners, we are spontaneously acting on that assumption when listening to what is being said in accordance with the perspective induced by the speaker. As speakers, we automatically monitor what we say in accordance with what we assume to be the intersubjectively shared reality *here-and-now*. And we are in our everyday life constantly oscillating between the two poles of the interpersonal coordinate of intersubjectivity, i.e. between the role of the speaking I and that of the listening you of Figure 1, p. 36.

Wittgenstein's comment that language is *'habit and institution'* (Wittgenstein 1968, p. 108) thus conveys a profound insight into the fundamental complementarity inherent in acts of verbal communication *as such*. And it is fully corroborated by our genuine bewilderment and complete lack of understanding of what is happening when we suddenly encounter a complete collapse of intersubjectivity: what George Herbert Mead called *'taking the attitude of the other'* (Mead 1950) constitutes such a basic and pervading feature of normal social interaction that it remains entirely inaccessible to the reflective consciousness of the speaker I and the listening you.

In order to explore the habitual and institutionalized aspects of complementarity somewhat further, let us therefore transplant the allegedly incoherent segment of the schizophrenic's story about the party into an entirely different setting. This time, we are listening to *a poet* as he is reciting

(IV O') I too was invited,
        I went to the ball . . .
        and it rolled
        and rolled away . . .

Our immediate reactions are on this occasion—even though in some respects probably slightly divergent—entirely devoid of the kind of bewilderment we experienced when listening to the incoherent story. When asked what is conveyed by (IV O') as part of a poem, some of us may perhaps answer that we honestly do not quite know. Others may express a feeling of having grasped its meaning intuitively and emotionally, without being able to put it into words.

Still others may venture to verbalize what they feel has been conveyed to them by the poet. They may maintain, for instance, that he has managed to portray conditions of human existence when our grip of 'ordinary reality' is wavering because we discover that things are not what we firmly expected them to be.

Literary critics may very likely agree to such an interpretation, arguing that the pun in this case serves to induce a genuine duality of cognitive perspectives. This duality, moreover, is introduced the moment we have heard and understood '. . . and it rolled', and it may be said to constitute a central aspect of the poetically established *here-and-now* at that moment: listening on premises laid down by the poet, we are thus temporarily able to share the feeling of alienation he wants to convey. What is subsequently said about rolling away is hence comprehended metaphorically. And what we encountered as a frightening loss of control of 'reality' in the schizophrenic's story about real events has thus in the poetic context been transformed so as to become accessible to our imagination. If so, it is in a certain sense made known—and possibly even to people who have themselves hardly ever before adopted the particular perspective of alienation induced by the poet.

The poetic context can accordingly not be fully understood unless we explore its foundation in contracts (or meta-contracts) of communication tacitly endorsed by the poet and his audience. In order to account for the two radically different 'readings' of (IV O), we have to conceive of the two different communication settings as embedded in different kinds of *language games*. '*Les sous-entendues*' are strikingly different on the two occasions: the narrative about the party is a game in which severe constraints are imposed upon shifts of perspective, whereas the poet invites us to engage in an imaginative play with possible worlds and potentialities of human experience. The opening of a book of poetry is thus in some important respect a ritual act: as we are putting aside the newspaper and are picking up the book of poetry, our habitual commitment to an unequivocally shared and conventionally categorized social world is abolished. Our decision to read poems implies a decision 'to do something different', i.e. to engage in a different kind of language game.

Consider, thus, what may happen when newspaper headlines about, for example, the war in Vietnam, increase in sales of cosmetics, famine in India and stabilization of the European stockmarket are brought together in a collage poem. Since we assume that the poet wants to convey something over and beyond what is made known by professional news reporters, our habitual and desensitized orientation towards daily mass media novelties is immediately abolished. To the extent that the author indeed has constructed the collage on that assumption, our expectation is institutionally founded and essentially correct. It is, moreover, *eo ipso* self-fulfilling.

The intersubjectively established topics of the collage poem are thus no longer merely those of the headlines as we encounter them on the front page of a newspaper. The moment the text is encountered in a *here-and-now* as defined by a poet-to-reader-of-poetry coordinate of interpersonal communication, the very architecture of intersubjectivity becomes a different one. As readers of poetry we may, for instance, temporarily be resensitized: being made aware of how distant social events have become part of our fragmentary and compart-mentalized 'ordinary reality', we may even for a while adopt a genuinely tragic perspective on our own docile and trivial mode of existence as well-informed citizens of the world. When reading the collection of newspaper headlines *qua* poetry we are then actually engaged in a game which—even though itself mastered as 'habit and institution'—aims at emancipation from a conven-tionally categorized social world.

The main lesson to be learned from our hypothetical experiments on transplantation of 'texts' is thus very simple: what is made known is in each case dependent upon what kind of meta-contract of communication has been tacitly and reciprocally endorsed. It can, accordingly, *not* be assessed by extrapolation from 'the text' *in vacuo* as, for example, some self-contained propositional content in contrast to what is already publicly assumed to be the case. In order to assess message structure, we have to examine the interpersonal coordinate of the act of communication in terms of reciprocally endorsed premises. The basis for intersubjectivity thus often seems to reside in what Ducrot has called 'l'implicité de l'enoncé'. And it is unreflectively taken for granted by the participants in the communicative act unless brought to the foreground by questions such as *'De quel droit dis-tu cela?'* or *'Pourquoi dis-tu cela?'* (Ducrot 1972, p. 8).

This implies, in turn, that we have to inquire into intentionalities and reciprocally presupposed intentions on the part of the I and the you engaged in the act of communication. The general paradigm of complementarity thus allows for an infinite number of variants. In the case of poetry, for instance, we encounter a whole variety of genres. Within one such genre, moreover, an impressive variety of individual variants may be distinguished. The generally acknowledged *'poetic freedom'* must hence in part be conceived of as a legitimation of a variety of architectures of intersubjectivity, i.e. as *in-stitutionalized deviance from other, 'ordinary' language games*, and accordingly also institutionalized acceptance of certain kinds of ambiguity.

We have already argued that poetic transcendence of 'ordinary reality' presupposes mastery of the semantic potentialities inherent in ordinary, non-poetic language. Such mastery implies capacity for decentration and—from the point of view of the symbolic interactionism of George Herbert Mead—also capacity to adopt the perspective of 'the generalized other'. *Adult semantic competence must hence be conceived of as a repertoire of interrelated, linguistically mediated modes of cognition and cognitive–emotive perspectives rather than, for example, a standard set of rules for literal language use.* And such a notion of basic semantic competence will be further elaborated when we later explore the role of general semantic rules within the architecture of intersub-jectivity.

Basic semantic competence and a capacity to adopt the perspective of 'the generalized other', however, do not suffice to account for our reading of the newspaper headlines as news and the collage poem as poetry. Spontaneous and contextually appropriate interpretation in such different settings testifies, in addition, to *a generalized capacity to adopt the perspectives of different 'others'*. And what is implied by a capacity to adopt the perspective of 'the generalized other' as opposed to a generalized capacity to adopt the perspectives of different 'others' may be further explored in computer simulation of human communication (see Bråten 1973). Anticipatory decoding may thus in a simulation programme be defined as involving simulation of self in the other's situation, i.e. the speaker may ponder: what would *I* take for granted if I were 'in his shoes'? He will in that case act on assumed similarity: his speech is monitored on the premises of the listener, provided that the latter is similar to himself. The generalized other is thus, in a way, a projection of self.

But anticipatory decoding may also be conceived of as simulation of the other in the sense that the listener's temporary social reality is inferred on the basis of the speaker's knowledge of what the listener thinks and feels in other situations. The speaker may in that case be said to act on assumed uniqueness, i.e. he assumes at the very outset that the listener is different from himself. It may hence make sense to conceive of simulation of self *versus* simulation of other in terms of individual differences, as characteristics of 'autistic' as opposed to 'other-oriented' communicators.

The generalized capacity to adopt the perspectives of different 'others', however, appears to be a *sine qua non* in institutionalized settings involving asymmetries of various kinds, such as, for example, that between an entertainer and his audience, the poet and his readers, and the lecturer and his students. Different subsets of meaning potentials are then brought into action, depending upon what is tacitly and reciprocally taken for granted as a shared social reality in each particular situation. Which semantic potentialities will become intersubjectively realized depends upon situationally and institutionally determined premises for communication, i.e. upon the reciprocally presupposed *'sous-entendues'* on different occasions. Making sense of what is said or written thus necessarily implies integration of what is mediated by verbal means into a more inclusive pattern of interaction in which the receiver is engaged at that moment.

In order to gain some insight into the subtle interplay between what is said and what is taken for granted we are therefore forced to transcend the traditional paradigms of substitution within linguistics and literary text analysis. These paradigms are all intralinguistic, i.e. one segment of discourse is being replaced by another in order to examine similarities and differences between the two. Contractual and partly institutionalized aspects of intersubjectivity are in such an analysis of secondary concern—if of any concern at all. In order to bring such aspects into focus, we have to engage in systematic substitutions of components of the *I–you coordinate* of the act of communication (see Figure 1, p. 36).

Šklovskij (1971, p. 47) maintains that the artistic aspect of a particular text, i.e. what makes us identify it *qua* poetry, is a result of our mode of experiencing it. We have in our hypothetical transplantation experiments tried to show how shifts with respect to 'mode of experience' have to be explored in terms of different architectures of intersubjectivity. Thus, by replacing a news reporter by a poet, the interpersonal coordinate of communication and the tacitly endorsed premises for intersubjectivity may be transformed. The poetically induced *here-and-now* is thus different from that habitually established between the reporter and the reader of the daily newspaper—less 'public', more intimate and revealing, aiming at an intersection of more deeply personal and existential aspects of the private worlds of the two participants in the act of communication.

Let us at this stage make a brief excursion from newspapers and collage poetry to experimental investigations of the ways in which purely spatial orientations of participants in a dialogue may affect conversation. Moscovici and Plon (1966) recorded dialogues between French high school girls, each pair of girls being asked to discuss movies both of them had seen. In one experimental condition, the girls would be seated face to face, with full opportunity for gaze contact. In a second condition, they were also seated face to face, but with a screen between them so that they could not see each other at all. In a third condition, they were seated side by side, looking forward in the same direction. And in a fourth condition, they had to talk together back to back.

A systematic content analysis of all conversions revealed some unequivocal differences between conditions with respect to syntactic and stylistic features. The back-to-back and side-by-side conversations were syntactically relatively elaborate and similar to written language. The face-to-face conversations, on the other hand, were more cryptic and—as gauged against standards from written language—markedly more incomplete. And visual contact appeared to be of hardly any significance under these conditions: what brought about informality of style appeared to be the spatially defined face-to-face orientation as such.

It is tempting, therefore, to extrapolate from Moscovici and Plon's inquiries into the relationships between purely spatial orientations and aspects of social distance to institutionally defined differences between communication settings. The face-to-face, side-by-side and back-to-back conditions may in fact be conceived of as ordered along a dimension extending from *interpersonal intimacy* to *social distance*. And the poet-to-reader-of-poetry setting resembles in that respect the second face-to-face condition in the experiment by Moscovici and Plon: the poet, even though invisible, is in a sense addressing us 'face-to-face', tacitly assuming that *we* shall contribute actively in making sense of what he has to say, and hence under no obligation to be elaborate and complete in any conventional sense of those terms. The reporter-to-reader-of-newspaper setting, on the other hand, resembles more the side-by-side or back-to-back settings, depending upon whether he reports on experientially shared aspects of the social world or on events of which we have hardly any experientially based previous knowledge. In either case, we are tacitly expected to share his perspective as an observer of facts on 'public' and conventionally accepted premises.

The poet-to-reader-of-poetry setting may thus in a certain sense, as already indicated, be conceived of as a setting for institutionalized deviance from other, more conventional varieties of written communication. The poet is, *as such*, expected to reveal sensations, sufferings and potential outlooks on human conditions rather than 'facts'. What he wants to make known is *a priori* expected to be incomplete in a certain sense, yet located in an interpersonal sphere between him and his reader, and of personal relevance to both of them. What on the surface appears an enumeration of arbitrarily collected and conventionally labelled facts is hence, when read *qua* poetry, assumed to convey some more profound meaning. Taking this for granted, the reader immediately engages in an active search for such an intended meaning, and with a heightened sensitivity towards semantic potentialities which would hardly be attended to at all if the reader-to-writer coordinate were a different one.

By examining what happens to a particular utterance or a given text across variant institutional, interpersonal and situational contexts we are thus made keenly aware of the interdependency among the different coordinates of the communicative act (see Figure 1, p. 36). Which of all possible aspects of a text will constitute the topic and occupy the slot at the origo of the *here-and-now* may thus, as indicated above, in part be determined by tacit presuppositions concerning by whom and for what purpose we are being addressed. If we consider the entire set of basic semantic potentialities inherent in ordinary language as a common code of potential contracts, we may thus conceive of variant situational premises for intersubjectivity as *meta-contracts*, i.e. as *contracts concerning which such potentialities are intended and situationally appropriate*.

Roman Jakobson conceives of such situationally induced constraints upon semantic potentialities as linguistic subcodes and the switch from one set of premises to a different one as a meta-linguistic operation. He writes:

(Jakobson 1966, p. 351) No doubt, for any speech community, for any speaker, there exists a unity of language, but this over-all code represents a system of interconnected subcodes . . .
(p. 356) Like Molière's Jourdain who used prose without knowing it, we practice metalanguage without realizing the metalinguistic character of our operations . . .

The characteristic spontaneity and lack of reflectivity with which we switch from one set of premises to another are perhaps particularly impressive in variants of interpersonal communication such as sarcasm, flirtation, etc. Transition from one set of premises to another is then often signalled by gestures and paralinguistic features of speech. The sarcastic tone of voice conveys an immediately comprehended meta-contract of reversal: what is said is intended and understood as the opposite of what would have been made known if it were uttered in a 'normal' tone of voice. Gaze, gestures or paralinguistic features of speech signalling flirtation, moreover, may convey a meta-contract by virtue of which what is said is spontaneously comprehended as paradoxical, but in a playful fashion: what is made known must be conceived of as an intention to engage in sexual intercourse, and at the same time as a denial of such an intention (Bateson 1955).

Formally similar patterns of duality are frequently encountered in situations in which the interpersonal relationships between the participants in communicative acts are characterized by tensions, ambivalences and contradictory impulses. As much is then often made known by *how* something is said as by *what* is said, and solid silence may on some occasions be as revealing as talk. This is also often the case under ordinary conditions of interpersonal communication. Thus, Birdwhistell has given a particularly vivid description of what his mother managed to make known by persistent and sustained silence:

> (Birdwhistell 1971, p. 52)... my mother was an expert on untalk—she could emit a silence so loud as to drown out the scuffle of feet, the swish of corduroy trousers, and even the grind of my father's power machinery to which he retreated when, as he said, 'Your mother's getting uneasy'.

Even instances of sustained silence are thus often 'perfectly understood'. Sustained silence may be brought about by violation of tacitly and reciprocally accepted premises of communication or by disagreement concerning such premises. If so, it will very likely signal tension and intentional disruption of active contact. On other occasions, however, it is immediately understood as a sign of deferential consent. Under still other conditions, a particularly harmonious state of intimacy and empathy has apparently been achieved when nothing more is being said. Different kinds of silence—some replete with, others entirely devoid of, embarrassment—may thus be intersubjectively established, depending upon whether tacitly and reciprocally endorsed contracts of communication have been violated, disagreed upon, confirmed or fulfilled.

In order to capture what is being made known about affective and interpersonal relationships and how such relationships are affected by what is said in face-to-face communication, we have therefore to inquire into an extremely complex and intriguing interplay of speech, silence, gestures and concomitant expressive behaviours. This subtle interplay of verbal and nonverbal components of social interaction constitutes a central theme in Birdwhistell's research on kinesics and context. Birdwhistell argues that what is preserved in typed transcripts of face-to-face dialogues is in fact only 'the cadaver of speech'. And an essential part of what is lost in the transcription has to do with what Roman Jakobson refers to as meta-linguistic operations, i.e. with shifting premises of communication conveyed by, for example, body movement, gesture, facial expression and tone of voice. What is made known by speech when it is 'alive' can hence, according to Birdwhistell, only be assessed by a joint exploration of the 'integrational' and the 'new informational' aspects of the entire, multifaceted process of interaction. And the integrational aspect is described as follows:

(Birdwhistell 1971, pp. 86-7) . . . the integrational aspect includes all behavioral operations which:
1. keep the system in operation,
2. regulate the interactional process,
3. cross-reference particular messages to comprehensibility in a particular context,
4. relate the particular context to the larger context of which the interaction is but a special situation.

We have tried to show how some such meta-linguistic operations can be conceived of as variants of a general paradigm of complementarity, i.e. how different premises for communication are tacitly and reciprocally endorsed depending upon variant institutional aspects of the interpersonal coordinate of the act of communication. We are writing on the premises of the reader, reading on the premises of the writer, speaking on the premises of the listener, and listening on the premises of the speaker. And we are engaged in all these activities under conditions of variant, though most often institutionally taken-for-granted or personally familiar I–you coordinates of human interaction.

The 'taking the attitude of the other' constitutes an integral, basic, and thoroughly intuitively mastered component of communication under such variant institutional and situational conditions. It can hence *not* be conceived of as one of a set of multiple meta-linguistic operations, i.e. as a relatively autonomous cognitive capacity superimposed upon linguistic competence. It constitutes the most pervasive and most genuinely social aspect of our general *communicative competence* as such, the common denominator of variant architectures of intersubjectivity across different kinds of language games, and hence the very pivot of those subtle operations by which comprehensibility in 'a particular context' and 'larger contexts' is achieved.

Our various case studies of dialogues, of alternative contextual settings for particular utterances and of transplantations of 'texts' from prosaic to poetic contexts may thus in retrospect all be viewed as illustrations of contextually determined variations of the same basic theme, i.e. as portraying 'tactically' divergent realizations of the same basic strategy. Consider, for instance, acts of communication performed under strikingly different conditions of pre-established commonality such as, on the one hand, the middle-aged couple brooding over their son and, on the other hand, the conversation about de Gaulle between the teacher of French history and his African student who has not yet learned about France nor about Western political institutions (see Chapter IV 1). We have in one case to do with communication within an intimately shared personal world, in the other with an encounter between representatives from entirely different cultures. What is said, however, is in both cases monitored in accordance with anticipatory decoding on the part of the speaker.

The premises for comprehension on the part of his listener are in the case of the brooding husband immediately and intuitively available in terms of a nearly perfectly shared social world and convergence of intentions at the moment of speech. In the case of the history teacher, on the other hand, the premises of the listener can only be vaguely and fragmentarily anticipated: his anticipatory decoding is based upon imperfect knowledge of modes of categorization different from, though related to, his own ethnocentric and habitually adopted perspective. The 'taking the attitude of the other' is thus essential on both occasions, only far more difficult, more reflectively controlled, and less perfectly attained in the latter case.

Consider, next, the marked but rather subtle differences with respect to premises for intersubjectivity and orientation towards ambiguities revealed in our two transplantation experiments. Such differences have to be conceived of in terms of entirely different presuppositions concerning *why, within how wide a range of potentially shared cognitive–emotive perspectives* and *at what level of intimacy we are being addressed*. And different answers to these questions are apparently institutionally taken for granted and, as it were, embedded as self-fulfilling expectations in different habitual modes of reading. The questions themselves are, however, hardly ever reflectively raised, not even on occasions when we rather abruptly put aside the newspaper and open a book of poetry or *vice versa*. As lay readers of various kinds of poetry and prose we are thus all of us ordinarily behaving very much like Molière's Jourdain.

What Apel maintains about prerequisites for constitution of meaning (see p. 43) must hence, when applied to acts of communication, be rephrased in interactional terms so as to take into account what Merleau-Ponty claims about 'sense-giving intention' and 'my taking up of this intention' (see p. 22). Making sense of what is written or said implies engaging in a social transaction, an engagement transcending that of 'an individual perspective' and 'a bodily engagement of the cognizing mind'. The boundaries of my individual world are temporarily expanded and opened to 'the other' on his premises, and an interpersonal coordinate of intersubjectivity is *eo ipso* immediately established. The I addressing me—even if anonymous—is at least in some significant respects tacitly identified the moment I am making sense of what I am reading.

Comprehensibility of written texts across the entire variety of genres of poetry and prose must hence be conceived of as due to institutionalized variants of the same basic paradigm of complementarity. Shifts from one set of premises for intersubjectivity to a different one are immediately induced by change with respect to the interpersonal coordinate of communication. What is made known by a given fragment of a text may thus be very different things, depending upon whether we are reading it on the presupposition that the author is a news reporter, a scientist, a poet, or a proselytizing politician or priest. Comprehensibility may be achieved on every occasion, though, thanks to our pervasive and intuitively mastered 'taking the attitude of the other'.

At this stage, however, some very important qualifications must be added. 'The perspective of the other' as intuitively adopted or presupposed by me may, first of all, be at variance with that actually adopted by the other—and at times even beyond his repertoire of possible categorizations and cognitive–emotive perspectives. Everyday communication appears in fact to be replete with erroneous presuppositions concerning commonality: we frequently address and listen to small children as if they were adults. Older people engage in discussion with representatives of a post-war generation as if both parts were able to adopt the very same experientially founded perspective—a perspective based upon the older generation's life experience of poverty, depression and the last world war. And many of us often make a nuisance of ourselves by talking to friends as if they were initiated members of our own quasi-secret scientific society, when, in fact, our professional vocabulary is totally incomprehensible to them.

Institutionalized genres of mass media communication, moreover, make for *imprisonment in self-fulfilling expectations*. The mere quantity of information conveyed by mass media is such that it can only be achieved at the cost of what Paul Valery (1951) aptly called verbal 'inflation': words and expressions which in our pre-mass-media society were reserved for mediation of experientially founded and intimately shared cognitive–emotive perspectives are being 'worn out' by extensive and *eo ipso* continuously more conventionalized and desensitized use. Our orientation as receivers of 'news' is thus characterized by habitual and institutionalized disengagement, and we tend to adopt the perspective of the impartial and disengaged observer even on occasions when the reporter happens to be deeply engaged in tragic events and in fact sincerely wants us to share his engagement.

Genres of written communication may also serve to freeze presupposed premises for intersubjectivity in such a way that the reader becomes insensitive to significant fluctuations with respect to such premises on the part of the writer. Authors of fiction may often more or less reflectively switch from one set of premises to a different one, and that may also at times be the case with those of us who presumably—as far as institutionalized genre is concerned—are writing on 'facts'. A writer may for instance in the latter case proceed most of the time on the general assumption that he is addressing a distant co-observer. When dealing with some particular aspects of his general topic, however, he may nevertheless tacitly take for granted an intimacy and reciprocally accepted tolerance of ambiguity of the kind encountered in typical poet-to-reader-of-poetry settings. A conscientious student reading every bit of Wittgenstein's *Tractatus* in a sustained and stereotype reader-of-analytic-philosophy spirit may for such reasons be at a loss when trying to make sense of what Wittgenstein has written about, for example, *residual silence* and *the I as a boundary of the world* (see Wittgenstein 1922, Sections 7 and 5.632).

Mismatch between what is *intended as presupposed by one participant* and what is *presupposed as intended by him* on the part of the other can only relatively unequivocally and with some confidence be identified as such by subsequent active interaction. Awareness of some misunderstanding at one stage of a face-to-face dialogue, for instance, may direct the attention of one or both of the participants towards potential discrepancies between them with respect to what has until then been taken for granted. The dialogue will in that case very likely take a meta-linguistic turn: as divergencies with respect to presuppositions are jointly acknowledged, a revised contract may be proposed and jointly endorsed. The disrupted dialogue can thereupon be resumed on reflectively and reciprocally confirmed premises.

Stalnaker defines presuppositions as 'propositions implicitly *supposed* before the relevant linguistic business is transacted', and he also considers the shared presuppositions of the participants as 'perhaps the most important constituent of a context' (Stalnaker 1972, pp. 388 and 389). Sharing of suppositions does not necessarily imply co-temporality of supposing, however. What by the speaker is supposed to be the case *before* his act of speech may thus under certain conditions become part of a shared social reality only *after* 'the relevant linguistic business' has been transacted. Contracts concerning what constitutes the temporarily shared social world may therefore actually be established by virtue of *initially erroneous, but self-fulfilling presuppositions concerning commonality*. Consider, for instance, the following case:

I am staying for a while with a friend in a city I am visiting for the first time in my life, and my friend is accompanying me on a guided tour through part of the suburban area in the vicinity of his residence. As we are passing a shabby and derelict-looking old building, he remarks:

(IV P) There was not enough profit from the production.

My friend acts in this case as if I already knew that the building we are passing is a derelict factory, whereas in fact I don't know whether it is a storehouse of some sort, an old-fashioned and forlorn apartment building or a factory until I have understood what he has said. What by my friend is erroneously supposed at the moment of his act of speech as pre-established commonality with respect to an experientially shared *here-and-now* is thus not induced as part of our temporarily shared social reality until the moment I have made sense of his remark.

Such subtle interrelationships between what is said and categorization of what is seen in the communication situation have been explored in a series of experiments on recall of utterances and pictures (Rommetveit *et al.* 1971, Blakar and Rommetveit 1974). Utterances are then presented in pictorially provided contexts. One of the aims of these exploratory studies is to examine how contracts prescribing particular interpretations of an extralinguistic setting can be embedded in what is said. And the findings testify to rather subtle and indirect modes of control of the intersubjectively established *here-and-now* of the act of speech: the speaker may in fact prescribe how to categorize significant aspects of the situation so as to transform it into a shared social reality without assuming responsibility for having said anything about it. Contracts securing a shared perspective on what is seen by both participants may thus be tacitly and reciprocally endorsed on the premises of the speaker, yet in such a way that he at the same time profits from 'the efficiency of language' and 'the innocence of silence' (see Ducrot 1972, p. 12).

Such subtle *self-fulfilling aspects of verbal communication* can only be fully understood in the light of what previously has been said about the relationship between directionality and control and the genuinely complementary relationship between speaking and listening (see p. 55): listening on the premises of the speaker also implies adopting cognitive perspectives on extralinguistic aspects of the situation which make his utterance comprehensible. Definite constraints are thus imposed upon potential interpretations of that situation, and an initially multifaceted, ambiguous and cognitively unstructured extralinguistic setting may be immediately 'disambiguated' by the act of speech. Which of an entire range of potential aspects is to be focused upon and intersubjectively taken for granted is in such cases indirectly proposed by the speaker— sometimes indeed erroneously assumed as an aspect already jointly attended to —and tacitly accepted by the listener the moment he engages in communication on the speaker's premises.

Our 'taking the attitude of the other' may thus very often be based upon adventurous, dubious and even definitely erroneous assumptions concerning convergence of perspectives and commonality with respect to interpretation ('*Interpretationsgemeinschaft*'). It is nevertheless—even under such conditions—a prerequisite for intersubjectivity. And in order to corroborate such an apparently paradoxical claim, we shall make some excursions from the more general issue of the relationship between what is said and what is *eo ipso* taken for granted. Let us first very briefly touch upon self-fulfilling assumptions concerning what is not written, but intersubjectively presupposed in fiction and poetry and, secondly, comment upon the role of erroneously assumed commonality from the point of view of language acquisition and socialization processes.

The capacity to profit from the efficiency of language and the innocence of silence is perhaps most clearly revealed in fiction and poetry in cases when there is nearly perfect consensus with respect to what the author has managed to convey to us 'between the lines'. A particular atmosphere or a contagious mood may for instance be induced as a dominant and distinctive feature of the intersubjectively established *here-and-now* of a passage of a novel or in a poem even though nothing has been written about that atmosphere nor that mood *as such*. The poet may thus describe, for example, a rural scenery or even a city slum, yet what essentially and unequivocally is being conveyed to us may be an unmistakingly tranquil experience of identity and 'feeling at home in the world'. A cryptic description of fragments of 'the real world' is in such a case comprehensible if and only if we adopt a particular cognitive–emotive perspective, and the author's own internally provided premises at the moment of writing are hence apparently imposed upon us via his description of fragments of the external world. The creative artist is on such occasions tacitly controlling significant aspects of our temporarily shared social world in indirect ways, in principle similar to those by which my friend's erroneous assumption concerning pre-established commonality came true, only more subtle and at times very reflectively and deliberately mastered.

When turning to issues of language acquisition, cognitive development and socialization, on the other hand, we have to consider self-fulfilling aspects of acts of communication within a more global, ontogenetic perspective. Decentration and socialization are in every society prescribed on culturally inherited 'adult' premises. And self-fulfilling, initially erroneous expectations concerning commonality across generations constitute for that reason an essential and pervading feature of the socialization process: the child's growing capacity for decentration is developed and monitored on adult premises for intersubjectivity as his initial egocentric orientation is constantly disconfirmed in transactions with adults. Communication failures due to disconfirmation of egocentric orientations necessitate *accommodation*, i.e. the development of novel and potentially shared strategies of categorization by which objects and events can be identified and talked about 'objectively' and within intersubjectively established frames of reference (see Smedslund 1964). Some erroneously assumed commonality—erroneously assumed on the premises of the parent generation—is hence required in order for real commonality to be achieved. And acquisition of adult semantic competence must accordingly be conceived of as increasingly abstract and linguistically monitored mastery of an expanding repertoire of interrelated and potentially shared modes of categorization and cognitive–emotive perspectives.

We claimed that the entire set of basic semantic potentialities inherent in ordinary language for that reason may be thought of as constituting a common code of contracts concerning potentially shared strategies of categorization and cognitive–emotive perspectives on what is being talked about. Institutionally, ritually and situationally different sets of premises for intersubjectivity were accordingly conceived of as meta-contracts, i.e. as tacitly and reciprocally endorsed presuppositions concerning which more restricted subset of potentialities is situationally appropriate and actually intended within a given, more inclusive, context of social transactions. Considering an act of speech as a move within some kind of game, we have thus to know something about which kind of game is going on in order to assess what is being achieved by that particular move. And in order to assess the entire range of semantic potentialities inherent in some segment of speech we have indeed to examine what is conveyed by that segment under conditions of different reciprocally endorsed meta-contracts.

Let us therefore at this stage engage in a somewhat more thorough and detailed examination of premises for intersubjectivity, meta-contracts and contracts. The necessity of such an approach has hopefully been demonstrated by hypothetical transplantations of texts. We were at that stage primarily concerned with gross and as yet only vaguely identified differences with respect to architecture of intersubjectivity, however, and such differences were in part revealed in different presuppositions concerning, for example, level of intimacy and orientation towards ambiguities. Being engaged in an exploration of institutionally determined meta-contracts concerning such aspects, moreover, we did not examine in more detail how different subsets of semantic potentialities inherent in any particular segment of an utterance or a written text were brought into action in different interpersonal settings. Let us therefore now try to explore the interplay of meta-contracts and semantic potentialities as revealed in particular acts of speech embedded in very familiar contexts of human interaction.

Consider, first, a word such as DEMOCRACY and how distinctively different subsets of its entire range of semantic potentialities are spontaneously presupposed as the intended and contextually appropriate cognitive–emotive perspectives in different situations. In one case, I am listening to *a patriotic speech* on our National Independence Day. The prevailing atmosphere is one of festivity and consolidation of patriotic feelings. The speech as such constitutes an integral part of a traditional ritual of celebration, and the speaker concludes in an enthusiastic voice:

(IV Q) DEMOCRACY, taken together with Christianity, is the genuine realization of the essence of human society and human mind.

(IV R) As good Norwegians, we shall always remain devoted to DEMOCRACY.

On an entirely different occasion, I am attending *an academic lecture* on different electoral systems in Western Europe. And the lecturer, a professor of political science, says:

(IV S) In order to assess the legal foundations of Western European variants of DEMOCRACY, we have to examine each country's constitution.

It may be extremely difficult to determine and compare the 'readings' of DEMOCRACY in these contexts in detail and with a reasonable degree of confidence, and it may even prove nearly impossible to achieve full consensus with respect to criteria by which the validity of such semantic inferences could be gauged. We may hence feel tempted to withdraw into formalistic escapism of some sort: in view of Lakoff's general assumption concerning use of natural language and reasoning, for instance, we may argue that (IV Q) and (IV R) constitute exceptional instances when use does *not* involve reasoning, whereas (IV S) may be conceived of as portraying a particular propositional (i.e. implicational) form. An analysis of logical form and semantic features is hence feasible only in the latter case, we may claim.

The implication of such a withdrawal, however, is simply a programme for semantic analysis whereby the entire scientific enterprise is reduced to a matching of a minute and highly selected subset of what is said and written against poorly understood propositional forms of dubious relevance even to such a very restricted sample of language use. How drastically Procrustean the resultant programme for research would be is brought to our attention by the fact that nearly all everyday uses of a word such as DEMOCRACY would evade analysis. And many an excerpt from presumedly scientific texts would most likely suffer a similar fate. Consider, thus, the resemblance between the use of DEMOCRACY in (IV Q) and Lakoff's use of the expression NATURAL LOGIC in the following context (Lakoff 1972, p. 648):

(IV T) NATURAL LOGIC, taken together with linguistics, is the empirical study of the nature of human language and human reasoning.

What appears to be conveyed in each case is indeed as much love and enthusiasm as reasoning: as DEMOCRACY is dear to the patriotic speaker, so is NATURAL LOGIC dear to Lakoff. A critical and reasoning reader may hence from (IV T) infer what Lakoff might very likely have said next if, instead of writing a serious article, he were addressing an audience of generative semanticists engaged in informal celebration of their independence from the tyranny of deep syntactic structures:

(IV U) As good semanticists, we shall always remain devoted to NATURAL LOGIC.

Something may thus obviously be made known even in cases when what is actually said or written deviates markedly from the ideal of propositional constellations of neo-Platonic concepts. And *what* is made known under such imperfect conditions may even be partly disclosed by very familiar procedures: what is conveyed by the word DEMOCRACY in (IV Q), (IV R) and (IV S) as well as by NATURAL LOGIC in (IV T) may indeed be explored by means of traditional paradigms of substitution. A first step may then be to consult dictionaries and examine lexical explications and indications concerning potential synonymities. This proves rather futile in the case of NATURAL LOGIC, however: the expression has apparently not yet been acknowledged as worthy of its own entry on a par with expressions such as, for example, 'natural history' and 'natural logarithm'. For DEMOCRACY, however, a variety of explications are offered. The following stems from *Webster's Third New International Dictionary*:

> . . . a form of government in which the supreme power is vested in the people and exercised by them indirectly through a system of representation and delegated authority in which the people choose their officials and representatives at periodically held free elections.

And at least *some* of the essential features of this explication may be condensed into briefer expressions such as GOVERNMENT BY THE PEOPLE and RULE OF THE MAJORITY.

If it is our purpose to *examine* rather than *prescribe* language use, moreover, verdicts must of course be delegated to the 'native speaker–hearer'. The range of candidates for replacement must hence be expanded on *his* premises. In addition to dictionary sources, we shall for that reason have to resort to maps of semantic–associative networks for the word DEMOCRACY based upon word sorting, word associations and other psycholinguistic inquiries (see e.g. Rommetveit 1968a, pp. 136–9, 1972c, pp. 64–70, Miller 1969, Rommetveit and Blakar 1973). Equipped with such an expanded repertoire of candidates for replacement, we must then find out which particular replacements are acceptable to the speaker as well as to his audience on premises of their own. With genuine appreciation of the intuitive nature of their semantic competence, finally, our inquiry must be conducted in a very unobtrusive way so as not to interfere with what is unreflectively taken for granted.

Some important features of the outcomes of such intricate empirical tests of substitution, however, may in the present case even be achieved by armchair simulation. I shall venture to predict, for instance, that DEMOCRACY in (IV Q) and (IV R) may be paraphrased as FREEDOM, LIBERTY and possibly GOVERNMENT BY THE PEOPLE, whereas for example both the latter expression and RULE OF THE MAJORITY will be acceptable replacements in (IV S). My prediction is thus that a reasonably selected set of potential substitutes after the test can be split into four subsets. Some candidates (such as FREEDOM) prove acceptable only in context (IV Q) and (IV R), whereas others (such as RULE OF THE MAJORITY) are acceptable only in (IV S). Then there will be some (e.g. GOVERNMENT BY THE PEOPLE) that probably prove acceptable in all three contexts, and finally still others (such as, e.g., DECENCY, RECREATION and DICTATORSHIP) of theoretical interest because they are rejected in all three cases. An empirical study would in addition allow for gradation of acceptability, showing, for instance, that FREEDOM is clearly preferred to GOVERNMENT BY THE PEOPLE as a paraphrase of DEMOCRACY in contexts (IV Q) and (IV R).

However, assuming such an outcome of carefully conducted empirical inquiries, what can be inferred about meta-contracts and semantic potentialities of the word DEMOCRACY in the two different settings, i.e. in contexts (IV Q) and (IV R) *versus* context (S)? What, for instance, can be claimed concerning common features and comparability across such divergent institutionally defined conditions as the patriotic speech *versus* the academic lecture?

What is being conveyed by DEMOCRACY in (IV Q) and (IV R) seems at first glance entirely undetermined, and such instances of language use have for some time been the victims of a strangely dualistic fate: while being relegated into the abyss of unreason by linguists and cognitive theorists of the Harvard–M.I.T. school, they were at the same time made the very focus of inquiry within the Illinois programme for investigation of verbally induced attitude change, emotive influence and affective meaning systems (see Osgood 1962). *Verbal communication is thus by one school explored qua pure reason, by the other qua pure affect.* And an entirely different scheme of analysis might hence be adopted as we switch from the academic lecture to the patriotic speech. Considering the latter as a case of purely emotive language use, we should abstain from analysis of semantic features and 'underlying conceptual realities'. Words and expressions should instead be examined with respect to location within an 'affective meaning space', i.e. in terms of quality and strength of the purely affective and attitudinal orientations evoked by them.

Various manifestations of this general dichotomy are also at times encountered in discussions on *stylistics* (see Prûcha 1972), and tacit faith in linguistically dichotomous reason and affect serves to legitimize and sustain sharp demarcation lines between linguistically based semantics and branches of literary analysis. Affect-signalling aspects revealed in propaganda as well as in poetry are at times conceived of as subtle and in some important respects autonomous components of verbal communication, i.e. as evading traditionally linguistic analysis of semantic features—and hence only to be assessed by some sort of disciplined empathy or by entirely different empirical techniques such as *Osgood's semantic differential.* The issue of comparability of use across distinctively different kinds of contexts such as (IV Q) and (IV R) *versus* (IV S) is hence, when viewed in this broader perspective, of considerable general theoretical significance.

The entire range of semantic potentialities inherent in a word such as DEMOCRACY can, of course, only be very fragmentarily assessed. What may be achieved by extensive analysis of previous use and intensive inquiries into semantic–associative networks of every participant in each communication setting is thus only a draft of a whole range of interrelated cognitive and cognitive–emotive perspectives. Yet one thing may be inferred with confidence: *the quality and strength of affective and attitudinal orientations are intimately attached to conceptual and associative potentialities.* Instead of components of 'pure reason' and 'pure affect', we thus encounter an intriguingly complex field of intimately related cognitive–associative–emotive potentialities (see Rommetveit 1968a, pp. 161–81 and 257–69, and 1972c, pp. 90–103).

What is being conveyed by the word DEMOCRACY is thus in each of the three contexts (IV Q), (IV R) and (IV S) only partially determined. The patriotic speaker and the lecturer will both—and legitimately—claim that what is being intended is *the opposite of* DICTATORSHIP. They will both accept a detailed explication of DEMOCRACY such as the one presented on p. 70), moreover, and the lecturer may indeed be perfectly willing to insert such an explication in his lecture as a definition before he proceeds to (IV S). The patriotic speaker is *not* willing to do so, however. Even the expression GOVERNMENT BY THE PEOPLE appears to be a little elaborate for his purpose, and it is probably accepted as a paraphrase only reluctantly.

When they are uttering DEMOCRACY, the patriotic speaker and the lecturer on electoral systems are thus both in some important sense—though admittedly for different purposes—'talking about the same thing'. The enthusiasm conveyed by the word in the setting of the patriotic celebration ritual is intended and contagious, but *contagion is being intended and achieved on semantically defined premises. What* is being conveyed can only be fully understod if we conceive of the particular acts of speech as embedded in a more inclusive pattern of social transaction. The speaker is firmly expected to address his audience as a member of a collectivity on an occasion when solidarity is supposed to be exhibited and reinforced. He does not fulfill his commitment as the public speaker unless what he is saying contributes to the ritually defined objective of evocation and consolidation of an in some sense ideologically founded collective euphoria. Whatever is being conveyed by DEMOCRACY under those particular conditions can hence almost as efficiently be achieved by ideologically relevant and semantic–associatively intimately related words such as FREEDOM, but not at all by only affectively equivalent expressions such as for example DECENCY or RECREATION.

The academic lecture, on the other hand, constitutes a ritual of enlightenment and transmission of novel information. The lecturer is *not* supposed to engage in demagogy of any sort: intersubjectivity is to be established in terms of expansion of shared understanding rather than ideological consensus and collectively induced mood. Utterances such as (IV Q) and (IV R) will thus—even though clearly related to his general theme—spontaneously be judged as situationally inappropriate by the lecturer as well as by his audience. Utterance (IV S), on the other hand, might very likely also be inserted in the patriotic speech, but then with a reciprocally taken-for-granted interpretation of DEMOCRACY as FREEDOM rather than, for example RULE OF THE MAJORITY.

Which subset of semantic potentialities will be induced is this in part prescribed by different general rules of the game in the two different institutional settings. There is in the one case a pre-established and reciprocal commitment to intersubjectivity on particular ideological, although admittedly diffuse, cognitive–affective premises; whereas the participants in the other case engage in communication on tacitly endorsed presuppositions concerning expansion and/or modification of shared knowledge. The I is on the latter occasion addressing the you as a less well-informed co-*observer*, whereas the interpersonal coordinate on the former occasion is one of interaction between co-*participants* in a collective social activity.

The basic *Why?* of communication is not reflectively raised at all, however, because the answer is on each occasion institutionally provided and tacitly taken for granted. Which meta-contracts have been endorsed can for that reason be reflectively assessed only by deliberate acts of violation, for instance when an engaged participant in the celebration ritual suddenly starts listening to the patriotic speaker as if he were delivering an academic lecture on governmental forms. The resultant state of alienation is in such a case quite revealing: what until then has been tacitly and intuitively accepted as premises for comprehensibility is by a temporary emancipation from the intersubjectively established *here-and-now* abruptly brought into the focus of reflective consciousness.

Merleau-Ponty's suggestive expression 'a certain kind of silence' and what he says about *transforming a certain kind of silence into speech* may thus be pursued in terms of empirical investigations of tacit, situationally provided and reciprocally endorsed meta-contracts and contracts of communication. Different kinds of silence may indeed be institutionally and ritually defined, as pre-conditions for meaningful interaction embedded in our capacity for 'taking the role of the other' in changing, though familiar, institutional settings. And such pre-conditions remain unknown to the actively and intuitively engaged I, whether speaking or listening, in the same way as water must remain taken for granted by—and remain unknown to—the fish swimming in it: presuppositions can become known only when we no longer unreflectively share them, i.e. under various conditions of alienation.

Some state of alienation is characteristic of the initial stage in any cultural anthropological inquiry into social interaction in which premises for intersubjectivity differ markedly from those with which the researcher is already familiar. Unfamiliar, but silently shared presuppositions thus constitute a pervasive—possibly also the central—theme of Lévi-Strauss in his search for the basic and pervasive *'l'inconscient'* (Lévi-Strauss 1971). Critics have accused Lévi-Strauss of having elevated the *unconscious* and *irrational* to a position of dominance and control in human and social life (see Corvéz 1969), but he may with an equal right be praised for having brought basic taken-for-granted and not-reflected-upon pre-conditions for human interaction cogently to our attention. Thus, Rossi maintains about Lévi-Strauss and the emphasis upon 'l'inconscient' in structural analysis:

(Rossi 1973, p. 43) The preoccupation with the unconscious is a preoccupation with discovering the basic structures which are common to the mental mold of the sender and of the receiver of the message, and which enable a genuine intersection of two intentionalities. In this sense, the unconscious is the only guarantee of objectivity of phenomenological analysis itself and the intrinsic link which would make of phenomenology an essential component of structural analysis rather than its mere external verification.

We are thus, by pursuing tacitly and reciprocally endorsed meta-contracts of human communication across institutional variants within a given culture and cross-culturally, encountering more and more thoroughly taken for granted and successively more widely shared pre-conditions. Such pre-conditions, moreover, constitute a very intricate problem area in which a variety of philosophical, humanistic and social scientific inquiries seem to converge. Wittgenstein (1962, p. 739) claims that any scheme of interpretation '. . . will have a bottom level and there will be no such a thing as an interpretation of that'. Hermeneutic philosophers of language are concerned with such a bottom level in terms of an unreflectivity taken for granted commonality with respect to interpretation, *'eine Interpretationsgemeinschaft'* (Apel 1965, 1966). Merleau-Ponty conceives of situationally and interpersonally established premises for a given dialogue as 'a certain kind of silence'. Lévi-Strauss' search for 'l'inconscient' may indeed, as suggested by Rossi, be interpreted as an attempt at explicating a widely shared aspect of 'silence', i.e. the common denominator of a whole range of situational variants. Social psychologists and sociologists, moreover, are faced with closely related problems in explorations of social origins of the self and the nature of social reality (Mead 1950, Festinger 1954, Berger and Luckmann 1967).

Contracts and meta-contracts of human communication, however—even though based upon shared ontological pre-conditions—also allow for variant architectures of intersubjectivity and even transcendence of pre-established commonality. We have already commented upon subtle self-fulfilling aspects of acts of speech, showing how initially erroneous assumptions concerning pre-established commonality with respect to categorization may come true by virtue of what is said and understood. What is left open and undetermined by the utterance *in vacuo*, moreover, is under ordinary conditions of interpersonal communication often spontaneously 'disambiguated' by virtue of what in that particular situation has been tacitly and reciprocally presupposed. Consider, thus, the following utterance:

(IV U) Here are too few chairs.

Imagine, moreover, the following situations. The speaker is a candidate for a political office, the scene is a room where a campaign meeting is going to be held, and (IV U) is said shortly before the meeting is going to start. The addressee, however, is in one case the janitor of the building who at that moment is standing in front of the closet where additional chairs are stored. In the other case, the utterance is made in response to an expected telephone call from the campaigner's wife. Being strongly engaged in his campaign, she calls to inquire whether her husband has attracted a large crowd. And we may even visualize a situation of mismatch between intended and presupposed I–you coordinates. The speaker, having picked up the telephone, may actually address the janitor whereas his wife may be listening to him on the assumption that he is talking to her; or the janitor may erroneously assume that (IV U) is addressed to him, whereas it is in fact addressed to the wife.

What is made known to the janitor is in any case clearly a directive or command. His interaction with the campaigning politician is unequivocally, though tacitly, defined in terms of a servant-to-master relation. When asked later on what was said to him, he may indeed very likely reply 'He asked me to bring more chairs'. The reciprocally endorsed presuppositions may hence in this case most appropriately be conceived of as a meta-contract by which some utterances in declarative form are spontaneously transformed into imperatives.

The wife, on the other hand, may upon hearing (IV U) immediately rush into the living room to tell the children 'Daddy has attracted a large audience tonight'. The meta-contract of husband-to-wife communication is thus on this occasion *not* that between master and servant, but firmly based upon shared concern with the political campaign. The intersubjectively established topic is for that reason neither scarcity of chairs nor the need to bring more, but attendance. *What is said would accordingly by both of them be considered true even if there were enough chairs, but crowded*: it is intended and immediately understood in terms of familiar and unequivocal metaphorical potentialities inherent in the expression 'too few chairs' rather than by a stepwise inference *from* scarcity of chairs *via* more people than chairs in the room *to* 'a large audience'.

What is actually said can thus, when explored *in vacuo*, only be assessed as an open and undetermined set of potentialities. What is made known may be entirely different things, depending upon what is tacitly and reciprocally taken for granted. A proper name or a deictically introduced '*he*' may thus remain entirely undetermined within the purely linguistic context, yet relatively unequivocally understood as '*he, as a politician*' once we know that the speaker is engaged in a discussion of candidates for a political office. What is being conveyed by an utterance such as:

(IV V) He is clever

may in that setting clearly be intended and understood in terms of a tacit and joint commitment to adopt only one among a whole set of interrelated and potentially shared perspectives.

This does *not* imply, however, that perfect convergence of perspectives is achieved. The two participants in the dialogue may indeed have somewhat divergent notions concerning what constitutes a person's capacity as a politician and which aspects of his personal qualities and achievements are of relevance to a political career. If so, there is bound to be some residual discrepancy between what is intended as tacitly presupposed and what is tacitly presupposed as so intended. The '*He*' in (IV V) is accordingly, even when 'disambiguated' by the tacitly endorsed meta-contract to talk about that person only as a politician, still only partially determined. What is implied by the meta-contract, however, is brought to our attention as we contrast 'les sous-entendues' of (IV V) with those of a conversation about, for example, driving skill or athletic competence: the partial closure of '*He*' implies at a minimum that he is *not* supposed to be referred to in his capacity as a car driver, nor as an athlete.

A main objective of our case studies in the present chapter has been to explore the ways in which what is made known by what is said is affected by what is tacitly taken for granted and *vice versa*. We have examined institutionally determined aspects of intersubjectivity in terms of characteristic differences between a poet-to-reader-of-poetry setting and other variants of written communication and in terms of meta-contracts characteristic of a patriotic speech *versus* those of the academic lecture. We have also tried to show *how* and *why* entirely different things may be made known by what is said, depending upon whether a master-to-servant relationship or pre-established convergence on to some particular topic is presupposed.

A very heterogeneous sample of 'streams of life' has thus been explored. And the interplay between extralinguistic conditions and semantic potentialities inherent in what is said seems, in retrospect, to differ in subtle and as yet only fragmentarily known ways from one particular setting to another. *The common feature, though, is clearly a basic contract of complementarity and reciprocal 'taking the role of the other'*, a feature whose fundamental and pervasive significance can only be fully appreciated in the shadow of traumatic breakdowns of the foundation of intersubjectivity in schizophrenia. The same general paradigm for investigation has hence been applied in every case: contractual aspects of acts of speech and written communication have been brought to the foreground by examining the fate of semantic potentialities inherent in what is said or written within different situationally provided frameworks for intersubjectivity. And now let us examine how such an approach differs from *the expanded Harvard–M.I.T. programme for analysis of presuppositions and propositional context.*

Part of what Birdwhistell calls 'the integrational' as opposed to 'new informational' aspects of language has traditionally been dealt with by grammarians in terms of *sentence modes*. The latter may indeed most appropriately be conceived of as modes of integration, i.e. as linguistically mediated contracts prescribing how what is said should be interpreted within the frame of interpersonal interaction in which it is embedded: it may thus be intended *to convey information* (in a *declarative* mode), as *a request for information* (in an *interrogative* mode), or as *a directive or a command* (in an *imperative* mode). Other variants have been explored by British philosophers of ordinary language, inspired by Wittgenstein's notion of language games. The verb 'promise', for instance, may be considered a 'performative' and in some important respects on a par with, for example, making the sign of the cross or any other ritually unequivocal act of promising.

The Harvard–M.I.T. expanded programme for semantic analysis may be conceived of as an extrapolation from the sentence *in vacuo*, via a revised theory of sentence modes, to a propositional grammar of communication. And such an extrapolation can only be achieved by expanding the linguistic analysis to 'silent', i.e. tacitly taken for granted, aspects of acts of speech. Outstanding proponents of *interpretative semantics* like Fillmore thus conceive of the 'deep structures' of sentences as containing silent verbs mediating sentence mode.

(Fillmore 1972, p. 20) For sentences whose utterances have the illocutionary force of asserting or informing ('declaring') there are reasons for believing that there is in the deep structure, *a silent illocutionary verb* of declaring having a first-person Dative NP, and having *the non-silent part of the sentence* as its direct object. (Italics mine)

Lakoff, on the other hand—being a proponent of *generative semantics* and 'natural logic'—maintains that silent performative verbs constitute part of the logical forms of sentences. He writes:

(Lakoff 1972, p. 560) ... it is claimed that the logical form of imperatives, questions, and statements should be represented as in (A).

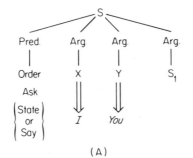

(A)

In (A), S_1 represents the propositional content of the command, question, or statement. Note that in statements it is the propositional content, not the entire sentence, that will be true or false. For example, if I say to you 'I state I am innocent' and you reply 'That's false', you are denying that I am innocent, not that I made the statement.

The interpersonal coordinate of the act of speech is thus split up by Lakoff into two arguments, and the mode of interaction between the two participants in the act is explicated in terms of the traditional trichotomy of sentence modes. What actually is said is then—after a possible, but presumedly sometimes superfluous 'I order', 'I ask' or 'I state' has been subtracted—also conceived of as an argument (or, in Fillmore's version, a direct object). And this residual part of what is said can finally, according to Lakoff, be examined in terms of propositional form and content as if it were an ordinary declarative sentence. His assumption is clearly that what is conveyed by ordinary declarative sentences, when uttered and understood as such, can be converted into composite propositional statements to which unequivocal truth values can be assigned.

We have already seriously questioned the latter assumption on the basis of the severe gains-and-loss account inherent in propositional analysis. What has to be relegated in such an analysis is not only unequivocal situationally determined variants of 'readings', but also significant interrelationships between the temporarily shared social reality of the I and you and what is said. We shall return to this issue, however, in subsequent attempts at explicating message structure. Let us therefore at this stage focus upon the 'silent verbs' by which Fillmore and Lakoff attempt to relate what is said to the more inclusive pattern of interaction in which it is embedded.

Consider, first, what happens when we apply Lakoff's formula for imperatives and statements in an attempt to account for the two different 'readings' of (IV V), page 75: *the political campaigner orders the janitor that there are too few chairs*, whereas *he says to his wife that there are too few chairs*. What has in this case been achieved by the insertion of different silent verbs for mode?

The formal representation of the imperative version seems indeed neither particularly natural nor logical. The campaigner and the janitor are engaged in meaningful non-verbal interaction determined by a tacitly and reciprocally acknowledged role relationship, and part of their conversation may hence be conceived of as incomplete fragments of a transaction which is replete with 'silent verbs'. What is made known by (IV V) may for that reason as unequivocally be conveyed by cryptic remarks such as 'More of those', 'More chairs', or only 'Chairs', and the 'silent verbs' are in such cases rather, for example, 'bring' or 'fetch' rather than 'order'. The master-to-servant interaction, moreover, is strictly confined to segments of their conversation intended and understood in terms of reciprocal roles. If thus the politician should say to the janitor 'Here are too few people', it is clearly not at all intended nor understood as a directive to fetch more.

The 'pre-programmed' transformations of (IV V)—in one case into a request for more chairs, in the other into intersubjectively unequivocal information about attendance—do not become any more intelligible at all by postulating different 'silent verbs' in front of what is assumed to be the same propositional content on the two occasions. On the contrary: what is precluded in such an analysis is an examination of the subtle interplay of tacit presuppositions and semantic potentialities.

This is also brought to our attention and further corroborated in Lakoff's own analysis of particular cases, and especially in cases in which interferences are made about presuppositions on the basis of the propositional content of what is said. Let us consider one such case, namely the sentence (Lakoff 1972, p. 581):

(IV X) Even John came,

and Lakoff's claim that this sentence presupposes

(IV Y) Other people than John came.

His 'natural logic' is apparently in this case based upon the plausible, though by no means uncontestable, assumption that 'John' in (IV X) refers to a person rather than, for example, a pet animal. His analysis of 'the propositional content' is based upon that assumption, and the outcome of such an analysis is then apparently accepted as the premise for a next step in a chain of 'natural' inference: since John belongs to the class of people, the 'Even' in (IV X) leads to the conclusion that (IV Y) must be presupposed. The reasoning inherent in language use in such a case can hence, according to Lakoff, apparently be represented as a general rule of interference: '*Even X*' presupposes '*Other Y's than X*', '*Y*' being defined by '*x is a Y*'.

Consider, however, what happens when we apply such an apparently plausible syllogistic paradigm to some equally plausible contexts of interpersonal communication. Imagine two situations, for instance, in which you are listening to narratives about 'real events':

'. . . I had been living out there in the wilderness all by myself for nearly a whole month, and I had never yet managed to get a glimpse of John, the hermit. But the smell from my cooking that day did not only attract his dogs. *Even John came*'.

'. . . I had been terribly depressed that winter. At the time when the last remnants of winter disappeared, however, things changed. Once more I felt that life was worth living. Spring sunshine, my health—all the pleasures of life came back to me. *Even John came*'.

What is presupposed in the first narrative is clearly that John's dogs came. The presuppositions of the second narrative, on the other hand, are apparently that John's coming was pleasant and that other pleasant events had taken place as well. Lakoff's claim that 'Even John' presupposes 'Other people than John' is thus clearly falsified: in neither of our two cases is (IV X) uttered and understood on the tacit assumption that other people came. The fate of the semantic potentialities inherent in (IV X), moreover, is clearly different in the two different contexts. Very different perspectives have been induced on the two occasions: John is in the context of the first narrative being talked about as an additional and possibly unexpected *creature*, in some respects on a par with his dogs; whereas in the other case he is being referred to as an additional *pleasure* on a par with, for example, spring and health. Lakoff's erroneous claim that (IV X) presupposes (IV Y) therefore does *not* invalidate the general rule of inference that 'Even X' presupposes 'Other Y's than X'. His error must instead be traced back to his initial 'propositional reading' of (IV X), i.e. to *the fallacy of assigning 'propositional content' to semantic potentialities.*

Fillmore and Lakoff's formal device for integrating what actually is said into the more inclusive pattern of social transaction by means of 'silent verbs' also seems to preclude assessment of subtle and significant contributions of those silent verbs when they no longer remain silent but are actually uttered. Consider, thus, the sentence:

(IV Z) I state I am innocent,

and Lakoff's claim (see p. 78) that the segment '*I state*' is superfluous—at least as far as truth function is concerned.

It is certainly true that expressions such as 'I state', 'I order', 'I ask' or 'I promise' ordinarily cannot plausibly be questioned or denied: we cannot very well deny *that* something is uttered the moment we are listening to that utterance. Utterances such as 'I stated . . .', 'You did not say . . .' and 'I shall state . . .', on the other hand, may be questioned and at times even— unfortunately—falsified. Such expressions in the past tense may convey assertions of public responsibility for having or not having said something and they are, in principle, intended and understood as referring to past events. In the case of the verb 'state', these past events are clearly acts of speech, whereas, 'I promised', for example, refers to an act of promising, whether verbally mediated or not. And let us now, in view of what most often seems to be conveyed by 'I stated . . .', explore what under certain conditions possibly may be achieved by expressions such as 'I state . . .' or 'He states . . .'.

The latter expression may, for instance, be employed by a lawyer on behalf of his client in written negotiations between the two parties before the contro- versy is brought to court as a case of civil law. What follows after 'My client states . . .' can then *not* later on be used as legal evidence, and it may hence be considered a declaration of a position or move in a game rather than an assertion that so and so actually is the case. A similar evasive function may also possibly be served under other conditions. Imagine, for instance, (IV Z) as embedded in the following texture of human interaction.

Sam, whose brooding parents we have already met, is mixed up in a narcotics case. He has been at a party at which pot was smoked and presumedly also sold. His friend Peter is also involved, but he does not know whether Sam actually smoked pot at that party. They are both present at a hearing at the police station, but are later on informed that a charge will be filed only against the persons who sold pot. Sam is subsequently summoned as a witness in that case.

Act I. The hearing at the police station:

Police inspector (to Sam): Did you yourself smoke pot at the party yesterday?

Sam (to the police inspector): *I state I am innocent.*

Sam (whispering to Pete): You see, between you and me, I doubt whether the verdict will be that I am innocent, if I should be charged. It depends upon what is meant, what I smoked was a mixture of pot and some cheap and entirely harmless stuff, I guess. . . .

Act II. In court, Sam as a witness under oath, knowing that no charge will be filed against *him*:

Attorney (to Sam): You were also present at the party. Did you smoke pot that night?

Sam (to attorney): Yes, I did.

What Sam *makes known* to the police inspector in Act I is not all contradicted by what he is whispering to his friend Pete. Nor can we conclude that his statement of innocence in Act I and what he says in Act II are contradictory. The subtle contribution of '*I state*' in Act I must hence be conceived of as an evasive manoeuvre. Sam may in fact, if asked what he means by his somewhat queer and evasive reply, be prepared to tell the inspector what he whispered to Pete. But he will certainly feel more comfortable if he is *not* forced to tell more about it in public at this stage: he does not yet know whether people attending that party will be charged even for merely having *smoked* pot, nor is he perfectly sure that the kind of mixture of pot and 'harmless stuff' he smoked will be considered 'pot' as defined in the penal law. What he says to the police is thus intended—and probably also understood—as a very cautious move in a public game whose rules have not yet been clearly revealed. Being torn between the alternatives of *either* exposing himself in a way that may harm him *or* telling something that may turn out to be a lie, he tries in a way to profit from 'the innocence of silence' in a situation in which he is forced to speak.

We may hence, by exploring what kind of contracts and meta-contracts are embedded in dialogues at police stations and in court, actually arrive at conclusions quite contrary to Lakoff's claim: statements concerning innocence or guilt—whether preceded by 'I state . . .' or not—are indeed as a rule understood by representatives of the law as moves in a game rather than evidence concerning real states of affairs for which unequivocal truth values are assumed. I may thus as a witness and under oath be held responsible for telling the truth, the whole truth and nothing but the truth concerning what I have seen and heard, but I am never in that same sense held responsible for the truth of my statement that I am innocent when I am actually accused of a crime. *The rules of the game are such that I am in principle supposed to remain in ignorance with respect to that issue until the verdict has been passed.* Utterances such as 'I plead innocent' or 'I am innocent' are thus within certain contexts of legal transactions all understood as 'I state I am innocent', i.e. as acts of stating or declaring in which the speaker is *not* held responsible for 'propositional content' in the same way as, for example, a scientist reporting his observations or a witness stating under oath what he actually saw and heard on a particular occasion.

The issue of sentence modes and integration of what is actually said in the more inclusive pattern of social transaction in which it is embedded is thus an extremely complex issue. An expression such as 'I state . . .' may also at times serve as a meta-linguistic operation, on a par with, for example, '*Let us assume that* ...' or '*Suppose* ...'. Such expressions may under certain conditions, convey proposals for meta-contracts: the speaker may, for instance, want to engage his partner in the dialogue in a play with possibilities in a dialectic conversation in which both of them are supposed to adopt a certain attitude of evasion—or at least of noncommitment—towards 'real states of affairs'. And such premises for intersubjectivity may be reciprocally endorsed in theoretical discussions of scientific issues as well as in cases of ideologically loaded or political discourse.

We have at an earlier stage briefly commented upon the ways in which utterances may serve a dual interrogative–assertive function: I may state something, but in a hesitant way and with a concomitant interrogatory gaze. What I say may in that case be immediately understood as a quest for social confirmation as well. Such subtle modulation of 'modes' conveyed by gaze and paralinguistic features may be linguistically mediated by parenthetical verbs (see p. 17). And some particularly intriguing problems arise in connection with possible self-fulfilling aspects of social confirmation.

The problems are cogently brought to our attention in some experimental studies of communication in small groups (Festinger 1954, Schachter and Singer 1962). These studies show how individuals, under conditions of uncertainty with respect to their own capacities or emotive states, tend to seek company with others who are assumed to resemble them in some respects or to have suffered a similar fate. *Conditions of uncertainty may then, in a way, be transformed to conditions of social reality*: what initially is experienced as a diffuse state of excitation, for instance, may be labelled and identified as different moods depending upon how others who presumedly have suffered the same fate behave and label the state of excitation. An initially unidentified state induced by hormone injection thus become cognitively comprehensible to the person himself only when talked about within a framework of perspectives shared by other persons he believes have been given the same kind of injection.

The relationships between formal aspects of language such as sentence mode on the one hand and tacitly endorsed premises for communication on the other are thus extremely complex and as yet only very poorly understood. A picture theory approach of matching 'propositional content' against 'real states of affairs' is certainly both legitimate and desirable within certain contexts of scientific verification. It proves futile, however, under conditions of human communication when such 'real states of affairs' evade assessment except via social and verbally expressed consensus. And it is for that reason singularly awkward if we want to examine, for example, an ideological debate or a patriotic speech with the objective of assessing what is going on in such settings rather than merely for the purpose of passing a verdict of irrationality.

In order to assess what is going on we may then have to acknowledge and examine genuinely creative and social-reality shaping aspects of communication whose manifestations have partly been revealed in psychological experiments such as those by Festinger and by Schachter Singer. I have elsewhere

(Rommetveit 1953, 1970) dealt with two issues bearing upon verbal communication as related to constitution and change of social reality. One of them is the issue of *normative expectations*, i.e. how a declarative sentence conveying a prognosis of some future state of affair when uttered within particular institutionally defined patterns of social transaction is intended and understood as in some respects conducive to that future state. The other issue concerns subtle relationships between '*is*', '*should be*' and *intended preservation or change of man-made aspects of our social reality*. By stating that some novel form of deviant behaviour *is* a kind of illness or *is* a crime, for instance, I am *eo ipso* making known which of two alternative familiar perspectives on deviance *should be* adopted. And what I say may subsequently be confirmed in terms of institutional modifications or innovations.

The games of ordinary language are thus often very subtle and composite games, with multifaceted and fluctuating premises for intersubjectivity. A model of linguistic competence in terms of abstract propositional structures and invariant semantic features may still be useful, however, even when inappropriate as judged from the subtle meta-contracts and contracts of actual use: it may, for instance, allow us to reveal contradiction and disentangle presumedly 'propositional' from 'demagogical' ingredients of ideological discourse. The outcome is primarily an explication of anomalies, however: actual use is only indirectly described, as deviance from some hypothetical (or 'ideal') standard based upon an erroneously postulated separation of reasoning from affective orientations. And the fallacy of assigning propositional content to semantic potentialities can only be avoided by a radical change of approach.

Our persistent focus on *what is made known* when something is said rather than on individual *cognitive representation of 'sentence content'* also implies a change of perspective on psychological issues concerning language processing. The early Harvard–M.I.T. psycholinguistics, being founded on transformational grammar and *individual* (as opposed to *social*) cognitive psychology, was hardly concerned with architectures of intersubjectivity at all. Experimental investigations aimed instead at a search for manifestations of linguistically defined structures in individual performance. This is particularly apparent in early experiments on syntactic transformations and in hypotheses about 'syntactic footnotes' to 'kernel forms' of representation (see Miller 1962). Thus, since there appears to be no difference between them with respect to (propositional) content, active sentences and their equivalents in the passive voice were investigated with respect to differential strains on individual information processing and storage.

Other aspects of the active–passive option attracts our attention, however, once we acknowledge the basic 'taking the attitude of the other' inherent in acts of speech and expand the scope of inquiry of the dialogue. The option can then perhaps most appropriately be described as an option with respect to foregrounding and what is supposed to constitute the topic for sustained discourse. And these issues are very similar to those encountered in more recent psycholinguistic research on negation.

Just and Carpenter (1971) examined the English expressions *'few of'* and *'a minority of'* under experimental conditions in which the two expressions were clearly synonymous *salva veritate*, each of them being used to refer to only two out of sixteen dots. Observed reaction times in true-false judgments, however, showed that the expression *'few of'* made the subject attend to all sixteen (or the majority), whereas *'a minority of'* served to focus his attention on the two dots. And the resemblance between these findings and observations on use of active and passive voice is perhaps best brought out by expanding the discourse by anaphorical deixis. Consider, therefore:

(IV a) A minority of the dots are red. They . . .
(IV a N) Few of the dots are red. They . . .
(IV b) Bill hits John. He . . .
(IV b P) John is hit by Bill. He . . .

The observation that (IV a) directs the attention of the listener to the two out of all sixteen dots in front of him whereas (IV a N) makes him attend to all (or the fourteen) dots is thus also corroborated by rules for anaphorical deixis. What is referred to by 'They' in (IV a N) is thus (all) 'the dots', whereas 'They' in (IV a) refers to 'A minority of the dots'. And 'He' refers in (IV b) to 'Bill', whereas John is being talked about when 'He' is uttered in (IV b P). This holds true, moreover, whether the discourse is continued by the speaker himself or by his partner in the dialogue.

The difference between (IV a) and (IV a N) revealed in Just and Carpenter's experiments on judgments must hence be explained in terms of *different, though tacitly and spontaneously endorsed, contracts concerning what is to be the topic of sustained discourse*. And such different contracts are clearly also involved in the option of sentence voice. In order to make use of that option, however, some emancipation from immediate, experientially determined event structures seems to be required: events of the kind made known by (IV b) and (IV b P) appear to be spontaneously experienced as possessing an inherent causal–temporal structure that happens to correspond to the word order of the active voice (Michotte 1954, Heider 1958). Making the acted-upon element of the event the topic thus implies a decentered shift of perspective on what is being talked about, and the option of endorsing passive-voice contracts of communication is for that reason available only at a relatively late stage of language acquisition (see Turner and Rommetveit 1967a, b).

Mastery of sentence voice may hence, in view of what has already been said about decentration and the expanding repertoire of increasingly abstract strategies of categorization, be considered an integral part of an expanding communicative competence. Increasingly abstract premises for intersubjectivity can be endorsed by the child as his orientation towards objects and events becomes more and more emancipated from fluctuating subjective, egocentric engagements. Decentration is revealed in transformation of pre-operational via concrete operational into formal–symbolic modes of thinking, in a capacity to adopt perspectives on variant states of affairs in a multifaceted external world by which successively more invariant and socially shared aspects are brought into focus, and hence in access to successively more abstract semantic potentialities.

This transformation is reflected in developmental studies of a variety of aspects of language use, and also in studies of free word associations: associations such as MAN–MILKMAN and MAN–DADDY are at a later stage replaced by MAN–WOMAN and MAN–BOY. Associative networks mirroring a subjectively organized private world are thus transformed into semantic–associative networks revealing highly differentiated repertoires of interrelated and abstract strategies of categorization (see Rommetveit 1972c, pp. 80–9). The contractual aspect of intersubjectivity—once truly acknowledged in the shadows of pathological conditions—thus becomes a central theme in exploration of semantic competence as well, and even in studies of highly automatized perceptual-motor skills embedded as 'subroutines' in our general intuitive mastery of language.

The 'speaking on the premises of the listener', for instance, is cogently brought to our attention as we observe a fluently bilingual person spontaneously switching from one language to the other in accordance with presuppositions concerning which one of the two languages is mastered by the person he is addressing at that moment. It has also been revealed in extensive and careful experimental investigations of the ways in which voice level is monitored in accordance with actual and presupposed premises of the audience, as a rule automatically so as to maintain 'a speech-to-noise-ratio favorable to communication' (Lane and Tranel 1971, p. 677).

The pervasive and inherent complementarity of the act of speech constitutes a central issue even in experimental research on the psychophysics of speech sound. Careful studies of sound discrimination show that we cannot identify very brief segments of streams of speech merely on the basis of acoustic shape: 'Listening on the premises of the speaker' is indeed required in order to identify a variety of different acoustic shapes as instances of the same discrete consonant. Experiments on phoneme discrimination thus indicate that the listener seems to use '. . . the inconstant sound as a basis for finding his way back to the articulatory gestures that produced it and thence, as it were, to the speaker's intent' (Liberman *et al.* 1967, p. 453).

Our 'reading on the premises of the writer', moreover, is under ordinary conditions to such an extent 'habit and institution' and so thoroughly part of the skill of the fluent reader that it entirely evades his attention. It is possible to arrange particular experimental conditions, however, under which some genuinely selective or even creative processing is required in order to make sense of what is written in accordance with what is tacitly assumed to be the writer's intent. We may, for instance, study reading under conditions of binocular rivalry of letters, by asking a fluent reader to report what he sees when for a fraction of a second two different letters are competing for the same position in his visual field.

A series of experiments have been conducted in order to explore this issue (see Rommetveit and Blakar 1973), and the outcomes indicate how *the fluent reader indeed seems to be imprisoned in meaning.* He may, for instance, report seeing *either* the word 'cold' *or* the world 'sold' if the two different strings of letters are presented binocularly, one to his left and the other to his right eye. If, on the other hand, he reads the word 'warm' immediately before the rivalry pattern cold/sold is shown, he apparently no longer has a choice. Having read 'warm' immediately before, he will only see 'cold' and nothing else. And this is the case even when he knows that two different letters will be competing for the same position and is explicitly asked to identify the word that is unrelated to the preceding one.

The imprisonment in meaning is in this case clearly an imprisonment in the basic semantic potentialities of the word 'warm': comprehending 'warm' implies engaging in an act of categorization which, once we have reached the stage of formal–symbolic modes of thought, actually constitutes an integral part of a very abstract strategy. The latter may be conceived of as a temporarily induced cognitive perspective by which *both* poles of a bipolar attribute— 'warm' *and* 'cold'—are in some sense being attended to. It constitutes in fact the common denominator of all contextually determined variants of 'warmth', i.e. of warmth as attributed to persons and colours as well as to bathing water and climates, and represents hence part of a common code of basic semantic potentialities.

The fluent adult reader has thus, the moment he sees and understands the word 'warm' in isolation, endorsed a contract by which he is committed to an abstract, socially shared and linguistically mediated strategy of categorization. And his spontaneous resolution of rivalry conflicts is indeed geared towards reconstruction of potential, intended meanings. One particular pair of competing letters such as p/r, for instance, may be seen as either *p only*, as *r only*, as *pr* or as *rp*, depending upon which perceptual resolution yields *a word*. Thus, pop/por is seen as *pop*, pob/rob as *rob*, pone/rone as *prone*, and shar/shap as *sharp*.

The architecture of intersubjectivity may thus be explored from a variety of angles and at various levels of analysis. The social nature of language is revealed at all levels, however, even in highly automatized linguistic skill displayed in solitary performance under artificially created laboratory conditions. The 'imprisonment in meaning' revealed under such conditions thus corroborates Husserl's critique of Descartes (see Husserl 1964, p. 135). Meaning is attained only by transcendence of the individual mind; solitary reading becomes comprehensible only when conceived of as embedded in a genuinely social game; *intersubjectivity has in some very important sense to be taken for granted in order to be achieved.*

V

ON MESSAGE STRUCTURE

V. 1. Anticipatory Comprehension ('Vorverständigung') and the Logic of Information Theory

IN THE preceding chapter we have primarily dealt with pre-conditions for communication, inquiring into general foundations of intersubjectivity rather than assessing what is made know when something is said and understood in particular situations. We have repeatedly warned against the fallacy of assigning 'propositional content' to mere semantic potentialities, showing how entirely different things may be made known by the very same verbal means depending upon which meta-contracts and contracts have been tacitly endorsed and which social reality has been intersubjectively established at the moment of speech. In dealing with presuppositions, moreover, we have argued that they can be meaningfully assessed only *qua* features of the social world, temporarily and partially shared by the I and the you actively engaged in communication.

In order to assess what is made known, we have thus in each particular case to inquire into what at the moment of message transmission is tacitly assumed to be the case. Human discourse is often strikingly elliptic, but also at times 'proleptic' in the sense that the temporarily shared social world is in part based upon premises tacitly induced by the speaker (see p. 66). The term 'proleptic' was proposed by my colleague and friend Willem Hofstee, who in a personal letter explicates the issue as follows:

Let me take off from your example, p. 42: . . . 'And the dragon was very angry, and he wanted to kill her . . .'. Incapacity to decentrate on the part of the child is an explanation, but some qualification may be warranted. What would you think of the adult who says to the child at this point, 'Hey, wait a minute. Who is "she"?'. That adult, in my opinion, is playing a rather pedantic joke on the child, since he knows that 'she' is the princess. He is supposed to know, since there is always a high probability of there being a princess in such a story.

So our adult is behaving like a Harvardian, which sounds like a barbarian, and that is precisely the term which is appropriate here: to the ancient Greeks, *barbaros* was the person who did not share the culture, the silent presuppositions, the *'esprit de finesse'* or, in your terms, (temporarily) shared social reality.

Let me tie this in with another example. Today I walked with one of the psychologists here past the Mayflower cinema in Eugene, where Bergman's latest movie is being shown. He asked me whether I had seen it. I said I had not, and asked if he had. He said yes, he had. I asked him how he liked it, and he said 'I liked it very much, but Mary Ann did not'; without ever explicitly having 'made known' to me that he is married and that his wife's name is Mary Ann, that they went to see the film together, and a lot of other things—and (if I am correct) *without assuming* that I knew all this. His utterence was proleptic in that it triggered a search on my part for a shared social reality which in turn would provide a basis for understanding the sentence. Incidentally, it would have been barbaric and pedantic to say, 'Oh, Mary Ann is your wife'. To be precise, prolepsis here served to establish a relationship between his wife and me as persons who should at some time get together. My comment would have been a crude rejection of that implication.

What from an externally imposed or 'public' point of view may be considered erroneous presuppositions on the part of the speaker may hence often more appropriately be conceived of as *self-fulfilling assumptions by which the listener is made an insider of a tacitly expanded shared here-and-now*. He is made an insider precisely because that expanded social reality is taken for granted rather than explicitly spelled out. This is not only the case in everyday conversations of the kind described by Hofstee, but also in human discourse of an ideological or even presumedly scientific nature.[5] What is said serves on such occasions to induce presuppositions and trigger anticipatory comprehension, and what is made known will hence necessarily transcend what is said.

Such transcendence has been explored by humanistic scholars as well as by social scientists, but from very divergent angles, and so far with hardly any attempt at relating—far less at coordinating—their efforts. Humanistic scholars subscribing to a hermeneutic philosophy have argued that all understanding is based upon an initial commonality with respect to interpretation ('*eine Interpretationsgemeinschaft*'), and that what is made known in any particular case is most appropriately described as an expansion and modification of such a shared '*Lebenswelt*'. Linguists, psycholinguists and communication theorists, on the other hand, have in their inquiries into anticipatory comprehension focused almost exclusively on statistical properties, i.e. on sequential constraints inherent in natural language. *Modern information theory* seemed at one time to provide them with very promising tools for assessing such constraints—and hence for explaining and even measuring predictability and anticipatory comprehension. It was later on definitely rejected and replaced by the conceptual framework developed within transformational grammar (see Miller and Selfridge 1950, Miller 1953, 1962).

Students of literature have for very good reasons been concerned with how it is possible for readers to comprehend more than actually is written, and creative writers have at times reflected upon that very issue as well. Thus, Hemingway offers the following explanation concerning the art of omission:

(Hemingway 1970, p. 75) It was a very simple story called 'Out of Season' and I had omitted the real end of it which was that the old man hanged himself. This was omitted on my new theory that you could omit anything if you knew that you omitted and the omitted part would strengthen the story and make people feel something more than they understood.

Professional students of literature have tried to explain such 'feeling more than is understood' in terms of a 'circle of understanding' (or perhaps, more appropriately, a spiral) by which the initial comprehension is continuously enriched and modified by successive reading. And this 'hermeneutic circle', it is argued, constitutes the very essence of the art of interpretation within the various branches of humanities. Wellek maintains:

> (Wellek 1966, p. 419) In reading with a sense for continuity, for contextual coherence, for wholeness, there comes a moment when we feel that we have 'understood', that we have seized on the right interpretation, the real meaning. The psychologists might say that this is a mere hunch, a mere intuition. But it is the main source of knowledge in all humanistic branches of learning, from theology to jurisprudence, from philology to the history of literature. It is a process that has been called 'the circle of understanding'. It proceeds from attention to a detail to an anticipation of the whole and back again to an interpretation of the detail. It is a circle that is not a vicious, but a fruitful circle. It has been described and defended by the great theorists of hermeneutics, by Schleiermacher and Dilthey, and recently by one of the best living practitioners of stylistics, Leo Spitzer.

We have already briefly commented upon some of the features of Apel's modern version of a hermeneutic philosophy of language (see p. 43). We argued then that what he has to say about bodily engagement in the *here-and-now* as a prerequisite for constitution of meaning seems to be at variance with other pre-conditions for intersubjectivity such as capacity for decentration and for taking the attitude of the other person. Apel appears to be somewhat inconsistent with respect to these issues, however. While stressing the individual perspective and bodily engagement, he also maintains (1968, p. 169) that '... *every objective knowledge presupposes prior intersubjective comprehension*' ('*intersubjektive Verständigung*'). And he comments upon 'the hermeneutic circle' as follows:

> (Apel 1965, p. 247) Also the famous 'hermeneutic circle', according to which we always must have understood already in order to understand at all as well as to be able to correct our preliminary understanding ('*Vorverständnis*') by means of methodologically guided understanding,—also that is based upon the assumption that in humanistic grasp of meaning ('*geisteswissenschaftlichen Sinneverstehen*'), to speak with Hegel: the mind is by itself in the other.
> (1968, p. 170, referring to Peirce and his original version of the hermeneutic circle) A vague anticipatory comprehension of sense ('*Vorverständnis von Sinn*') is taken for granted, (a comprehension) which, to speak with Heidegger, mediates something through an anticipation of ('*Vorlaufen in*') potentialities of human existence and is itself further explicated ('*verdeutlicht*') by virtue of such mediation.

The terminology of Wellek and Apel is thus strikingly different from that of information theory: Shannon (1951) and Miller and Selfridge (1950) deal with redundancy of written material in terms of *predictability of words or strings of letters* on the basis of preceding words or letter sequences, whereas Wellek and Apel are dealing with transcendence of what is written or said in terms of *humanistic grasp of meaning and anticipation of potentialities of human existence*. Both approaches are nevertheless concerned with phenomena of ellipsis and 'prolepsis', however, and for that reason of considerable relevance in the present context. And let us now examine how what from a humanistic point of view is dealt with as anticipatory comprehension ('*Vorverständigung*') may be explicated in terms of the logic of information theory.

The main features of the latter can be exhibited by means of a very simple question-and-answer task. An object is located in one of the cells of a square consisting of 16 cells (see Figure 3). I know where it is, but you do not. Your task is then simply to find out in which one of the 16 cells the object is located, and you are requested to do so by means of questions that can be answered by either 'Yes' or 'No'. The dialogue may hence proceed as follows:

(1) *'Is it in the right half?'* 'No'
(2) *'Is it in the upper half of the left half?'* 'Yes'
(3) *'Is it in the right half of the upper half?'* 'No'
(4) *'Is it in the upper half of the left half?'* 'No'

FIGURE 3. Square for the question-and-answer task

What has been made known at this stage is that the object is located in cell X, and the entire dialogue can in this case be described as a sequentially arranged reduction of an initial state of uncertainty on your part. This initial state corresponds to the entire square in Figure 3: you know at the outset that the object is located in some as yet not identified cell of that square, i.e. that it may be located in any single one out of 16 cells. My first answer serves to eliminate one-half of that entire area, my second answer eliminates one-half of the remaining half of it, and so on. Let us at this stage deliberately ignore these purely quantitative aspects, however, and turn to the dialogue as such.

Notice, first of all, that *the word 'square' does not enter our dialogue at all, despite the fact that message transmission at every single stage is based upon the assumption that the two of us have the same particular square in mind.* We assume—correctly, and by a tacitly endorsed contract—that we are talking about the same square. This constitutes the initially shared, unquestioned or *free information* on to which your very first question is nested or *bound*. Whether I have shown you a visual display of the square or carefully described it to you in advance is of no particular significance in the present context. It constitutes in either case an initially shared social reality and a *sine qua non* for further meaningful discourse concerning the location of the object.

This is not only true of the unmentioned square, however, but also of, for example, *the right half of it* introduced in question (1)—or rather, *the left half* implied by my answer—when from stage (3) on it is no longer mentioned.

Notice, thus, how my answer at every successive stage is nested on to what at that particular stage has already been established as a shared social reality (or unquestioned, free information). Notice, furthermore, how my answer at stage (*n*) is tacitly presupposed in your question at stage (*n* + *2*). Both of us know—and know that the other knows—after stage (1) that the object is located somewhere in the left half of the square in Figure 3. This shared knowledge is a prerequisite for what is made known at stage (3), even though at that stage tacitly taken for granted by both of us.

Even more cryptic conversations are at times encountered when such a simple question-and-answer task is conducted in informal settings. Your last question may on such an occasion very likely be reduced to merely 'The upper?' or even a gesture such as an upward-pointing thumb accompanied by an interrogatory gaze. And we may hence from the present simple demonstration of sequential reduction of uncertainty return to our previous analysis of ellipsis (see Chapter IV.1). It is certainly impossible to account for what is made known in the conversation between Tolstoy's lovers and by the depressed husband to his equally gloomy wife in terms of bits of information, i.e. by extrapolation from what is said via layers of presuppositions to some well-defined initial state of uncertainty. What is 'perfectly understood' in such cases, however, can hardly be understood at all unless what is said is nested on to what is already assumed to be the case—and in principle in ways resembling those revealed in the question-and-answer game.

What is left of sequential structure in our dialogue when we leave out quantification is namely a particular pattern whereby novel information is nested on to what is already assumed to be the case. Consider, for instance, our initially shared presupposition concerning the square with its 16 cells. It is not only taken for granted as the set of all possible locations of the object, but also tacitly presupposed as the frame of reference whenever proper sense is made of words for direction ('left' *versus* 'right') and quantity ('half'). What is made known at one particular stage is thus not only made part of an expanded shared social reality, but serves at the same time as a prerequisite for making proper sense of what is said at the next stage. We have hence to do with *presuppositions which serve as bases for anticipatory comprehension as well.*

We have with our question-and-answer game shown how verbal message transmission under such specific and systematically arranged conditions can be described as a progressive nesting of information on to what the speaker and the listener by explicit agreement at the outset assumed to be the case. The game was arranged in such a way that what was made known could even be assessed quantitatively, in terms of successive reduction of an initial state of uncertainty. The dual function of every successive segment of the dialogue also remains the same, however, when my four successive answers are transformed into one single utterance. What was achieved step by step in the dialogue is then made known by:

(V A) It is in the lower half of/the left half of/the upper half of/the left half/of (the square);

or—in a more easily comprehended fashion—by:

(V A′) It is (in the square)/in its left half/in the upper half of that left half/in the left half of that upper half/in the lower half of that left half.

The exact location of the object is in each case made known by a particular pattern of nesting such that, in V A′, for example, what is made known to the left of each vertical line has to be taken for granted *and* as a basis for comprehending what follows to the right. The same pattern of nesting appears in (V A) also, but in the opposite order. This implies, more specifically, that *part of what is said serves as unquestioned, free information on a par with what in the dialogue appeared as tacitly endorsed presuppositions.* Other parts make sense if and only if *bound* to such *free information*, i.e. only when understood as contingent upon—and at the same time as an expansion of—an already established social reality.

Similar patterns of nesting are often encountered in narratives, for instance when the identity of some person is taken for granted by the narrator—and *eo ipso* intersubjectively established—on the basis of inference from what has been made known at some earlier stage. We may, for instance, hear about two persons, one old man and one young man, and the latter is subsequently referred to as 'the son'. Nothing has been *said* about kinship, the identity of 'the son' is made known only by implication, and we have hence a case of 'prolepsis' and anticipatory comprehension on the part of the listener. Gleason (1968, p. 55) considers such phenomena as evidence for 'a semological reticulum' which '. . . keeps ahead of sentence generation, though not necessarily far ahead'.

The immediate identification of 'the son' as the previously mentioned young man may in such a case also be described as due to a tacitly endorsed contract defining the entire set of persons jointly attended to within the *here-and-now* of the story (see Figure 1, p. 36). We noticed in the question-and-answer game how my answer at stage (*n*) was tacitly presupposed in your question at stage (*n* + 2). An analogous nesting appears in the narrative. Only two persons have so far been introduced in our temporarily shared social world. When therefore '*the son*' (by virtue of the definite article) is assumed to be known already, he has to be the younger one of those two men and nobody else. The range of possible identities has been drastically constrained, in principle in the same way as the set of possible locations had been reduced from stage (*n*) to stage (*n* + 2) in the question-and-answer game.

What appear from the general perspective of information theory as sequential constraints may hence, when we examine the architecture of intersubjectivity, be assessed as '*Vorverständigung*' based upon tacitly endorsed contracts concerning a temporarily shared social world. What is made known can then *not* be described in terms of any autonomous propositional content, not even in Chomsky's modified version of focus and presupposition. Message structure must instead be conceived of as a particular pattern of nesting, generated in an interplay of tacit and verbally induced presuppositions on the one hand and semantic potentialities on the other.

Let us now examine particular cases of such interplay in somewhat more detail. Consider, for instance, the following case.

Two men who live in the same apartment house meet in front of the entrance of that house, and they engage in conversation about the general prosperity in that neighbourhood. So far, all flats have been occupied by young couples. The day before, however, they had both watched a man appearing to be in his late sixties move into a vacant flat. And one of the two men at the entrance now says to the other:

(V B) The old man is poor.

Notice, first of all, the resemblance between (V B) and (V A') with respect to nesting, i.e. how in both cases part of what is made known has to be interpreted in the light of other parts. The word 'poor', for instance, is as such replete with semantic potentialities. It is only partially determined even if—as in the present case—said about a person and as 'the focus' of the sentence. The word may thus under other conditions serve to make known, for example, lack of talents or skill of some kind. Which general potentiality is intended by the speaker in that particular situation, however, is immediately comprehended by the listener: what is conveyed by 'poor' is unequivocally determined by 'Vorverständigung' in accordance with their temporary joint concern with the prosperity of people in their neighbourhood.[6]

What the speaker wants to make known (or assert) by means of that semantic potentiality, moreover, will not be transmitted unless the whole phrase 'The old man' is tagged on to the (presumedly already known) same person within a pre-established shared social world. And what is conveyed by 'old' is, of course, contingent upon the fact that age is attributed to 'the . . . man' rather than to, for example, a church or some object in a historical museum. Pushing the analogy with the question-and-answer game, we may thus consider 'The . . . man' as comparable to the segment (in the square) in (V A'), i.e. as an already established social reality to which whatever is made known by the remaining part of the utterance is bound.

The word 'old' serves as a further specification of 'The . . . man'. Such further specification appears to be superfluous in the situation described above, but may be essential in order to establish identifying reference under other conditions such as, for instance, if a young man were passing by and jointly attended to by the two neighbours at the moment (V B) was uttered. *The old age of the new tenant, however, is not asserted or made known in the same fashion as his poverty, but assumed to be the case and tacitly agreed upon by both men in advance.* The whole phrase 'The old man' can thus in the situation we have described be replaced by the deictic 'He' if that man happens to be the focus of their joint attention at the moment of speech. 'He' may be replaced by a pointing gesture, moreover, and we have then reduced (V B) to the kind of cryptic dialogues we encountered under conditions of nearly perfect complementarity and synchronization of intention and thought.

The act of communication in front of the entrance of the apartment house may therefore be described as a rather cautious and safe move in a language game firmly embedded in a pre-established shared social world. We assume, in such a description, credibility and mastery of communication contracts, including agreement with respect to the act of categorization implied by one of the semantic potentialities of 'poor'. Comprehension of what is said may in that case be considered an expansion of an experimentally established and confirmed social reality to a position at which that social reality is slightly expanded. Such a move is also relatively safe in the sense that very little is required in terms of capacity for decentration, imagination and adoption of abstract 'as-if' perspectives on the part of the listener.

Considerably more is required, however, if we are listening to (V B) as the opening sentence of a short story (or novel) by some unknown author. As listeners we have then to endorse a meta-contract, i.e. a contract concerning how to deal with the contracts of categorization implied by what is said, which differs from that tacitly endorsed by the two men. We must be willing (and have the capacity) to deal with abstract novelties *as if* they were already familiar, on the assumption that what is initially abstract, unknown and largely undetermined will become familiar as we continue listening. Comprehension is therefore under such conditions an adventurous and proleptic move into an imagined social world, and far beyond the capacity of mentally retarded people who have no problems of comprehending the same sentence in the new tenant setting.

The different meta-contracts in the two different settings may be vaguely described as a tacitly endorsed agreement concerning expansion of a shared social reality *versus* an equally unreflectively presupposed agreement concerning construction of an imagined social reality. If we want to push the analogy with the question-and-answer game once more, we may for that reason conceive of the tacit agreement between us listeners and the author of the short story in terms of a reversal of the game: the point of departure is one unknown cell of the square in Figure 3 which—being presented as if known—will later on be identified with respect to location as more and more of the area surrounding it will be made known to us.

This analogy, however, seems plausible only if we ignore the intralinguistic structure of (V A) and compare the relationship between the entire utterance and the experientially established social reality in the new tenant setting with that between the utterance and the remaining part of the story in the short story setting. If we examine what is made known within the utterance as an opening sentence of a short story, on the other hand, we are actually faced with a particular pattern of nesting of novelties strictly analogous to the progressive expansion of the shared social reality in the new tenant setting. Comprehending (V A) in the short story setting thus implies playing the game of presupposing that one particular man has already been unequivocally identified and that his old age is considered an unquestioned fact when it is made known that he is poor as well. The opening sentence of the short story is thus made up of a condensed nesting of presuppositions. What is achieved by such a condensed nesting as compared to, for example, the characteristically elaborate and slow-moving style of children's fairy tales, moreover, is some sort of initial intimacy: the author tries to make us 'insiders' of his imaginary social world by pretending that we are already at the outset familiar with parts of it.

The pervading theme in our analysis of the question-and-answer game as well as in our case studies of specific acts of verbal communication has been the nesting of novel information on to whatever at each successive stage of message transmission is known already or presupposed as already known. We have tried to show how such nesting can be assessed in terms of anticipatory comprehension, i.e. how what is initially unknown to the listener is made known to him in terms of a progressive expansion and modification of an actual or intersubjectively presupposed shared social world. In doing so, however, we have tried to exploit certain central aspects of general information theory far beyond its initial, proper, but restricted field of application, that of well-defined and even measurable states of uncertainty. And now let us examine how our expanded approach differs from that adopted by psycholinguists prior to the era of transformational grammar.

A key term in the early application of information theory to linguistic and psycholinguistic problems was 'redundancy', defined in terms of sequential *constraints upon strings of letters* or words as such, *in vacuo*. In retrospect, perhaps the single most remarkable feature of such an approach is the detachment of problems of sequential constraints from problems of meaning. A finite number of alternatives (such as the alphabet) seemed to be a prerequisite for measuring predictability, and hardly any systematic attempt was made at explicating the relationship between such presumedly statistical properties of language on the one hand and the interplay between intersubjectively established presuppositions and semantic potentialities on the other. What was assessed as conditional probabilities of segments of speech or written language was nevertheless focused upon as a possible clue to human linguistic skill and even at times interpreted as internalized knowledge of sound-and-word sequences (see Krech and Cruchfield 1966, p. 468). We shall argue, however, that it may be more appropriately described as a poorly understood experimental artifact, serving to conceal rather than reveal what actually goes on when a person sets out to guess, letter by letter, some entirely unknown sentence.

This can be shown in careful case studies of individual performances in such guessing games, and by comparing individual human performances to that of a computer guessing on the basis of nearly perfect statistical knowledge of conditional probabilities (see Rommetveit 1971). Consider, for instance, the following Norwegian target sentence and a literal English translation:

(V C) Nødsignalene /deres/ble /sett /fra /land.
The emergency signals /their /were /seen /from /land.

A computer guessing position by position on the basis of perfect statistical knowledge of three-letter sequences in Norwegian makes on the average approximately three errors per position, whereas students serving as subjects in the guessing game made on the average only two. Sequences which proved to be real problems for the students were easily dealt with by the computer, however, whereas the opposite held true for other sequences. The computer is thus far superior to the students in 'anticipating' the word 'deres' ('their'), making on the average only two errors per letter, whereas the students on the average made more than four mistakes. It has difficulties in predicting the final word 'land', on the other hand, making more than three errors per letter, whereas most students were able to predict that entire letter sequence without committing one single mistake.

We may, of course, expand and modify the basis for the computer's performance in various ways: it may be equipped with statistical knowledge of sequences of any length, and we may even replace the letter (or rather the position) by more inclusive linguistically defined units such as morphemes or words. Such modifications may improve its performance, but its strategy will remain essentially the same—and very different from that of the typical person engaged in the guessing game. Let us therefore, in order to spell out that difference with respect to strategy, briefly examine why some segments of (V C) were particularly difficult for the human performers while others created far more trouble for the computer.

As is generally the case in Norwegian, the possessive pronoun is positioned after the definite form of the noun. The suffix for plural definite ('. . . ene') followed by 'deres' is hence a relatively frequent combination, and for that reason easily disclosed by the computer. The pronoun 'deres' serves a deictic function, however, making full sense only when tagged on to some entities already intersubjectively established within the temporarily shared *here-and-now* of the act of communication. And no such persons have been identified at the stage of the guessing game when only the very first word of the sentence has been disclosed. The human subject is hence at this stage of the game at a loss: he is trying to reconstruct an intended message of which only a fragment has been made known to him, filling in what might plausibly follow in a situation when 'Nødsignalene' ('The emergency signals') and nothing else has been said. The word 'deres' would hardly follow in such a situation, even though a very probable continuation as assessed in terms of conditional probabilities of letter (and word) sequences across all possible intralinguistic contexts.

Consider, next, the situation when only the final word remains to be disclosed. What has been made known to the person engaged in the game at this point is that emergency signals were seen from somewhere. He has reason to believe—by 'prolepsis' from the deictic 'deres'—that the signals were emitted by *people* in danger, and he can within the constraints of his own experientially established social world most plausibly make sense of what has been disclosed in terms of some emergency somewhere along the coast of Norway.

What remains to be made known next is clearly, on the basis of what has been made known already, the location from where the signals were seen. And signals somewhere along the coast are most often seen from land. Reconstruction of the final fragment of the message is thus achieved by anticipatory comprehension, and on the simple and tacit assumption that the whole as yet unfinished sentence is intended to make known some event within a restricted world of experiential possibilities. Experientially founded plausibility is in this case at variance with conditional probability of letter sequences in Norwegian, however, and the computer's statistical prediction is accordingly at this final stage of the game far inferior to human anticipatory comprehension.

The rules imposed upon the guessing game are such that performance is assessed in terms of errors per positions. The entire set of letters (including the empty position) constitute altogether 28 alternatives, and purely random choice would hence yield an average of 14 errors. The actual performances by individual subjects as well as by the computer are therefore, when gauged against purely random perfomance, impressive. They may also be converted to measures of redundancy and compared in strictly quantitive terms.

What is concealed by such quantification, however, is the striking difference between the computer and the human subject with respect to strategy. We have already commented upon the typical human strategy at two different stages of the game, showing how *what is assessed as errors per position actually appears as the end product of an attempt at reconstructing an intended message.* This becomes even more obvious in an inspection of each individual case, and in particular when the subject is asked to comment upon his own incorrect guesses.

We discover, then, that the person engaged in the game as a rule proceeds to reconstruct the message word by word and at times—particularly towards the end of a target sentence—by anticipation of even longer sequences. Quite a few subjects were thus able to anticipate the entire final sequence 'fra land' in (V C). Such a general strategy appeared at times futile, however, particularly at the very beginning of the game and at particular troublespots such as 'deres'. Only on such occasions are there regressions to purely asemantic strategies such as, for instance, an apparently random procedure of guessing at letters in an alphabetical order with omission of those already discarded as incorrect as well as of those constituting phonologically illegitimate continuations.

The person engaged in the guessing game is thus requested to guess letter by letter, but his guess at one particular letter is in reality most of the time an encoding of part of a word by which he tries to anticipate *what will be made known next.* And his basis for such anticipation is improved as more and more of the target sentence is disclosed. This is cogently demonstrated when we expand the rules of the game and ask, not only for the next letter, but also general questions concerning what kind of topic he believes is being dealt with, by whom, and in what kind of a situation the target sentence has been produced, etc. His answers to such questions testify to adventurous, but in general successively more successful, 'prolepsis': those fragments of the sentence that at a given stage have been disclosed already serve as a basis for tentative, but in general progressively more confident, inferences concerning the intersubjectively established *here-and-now* as well as the I-you coordinate of the act of communication.

This is further corroborated by a careful inspection of individual errors. Nearly all of them are 'good' errors, sometimes based upon correct anticipations encoded in expressions synonymous with those of the target sentence, and on other occasions aimed at an encoding of different, though related and equally plausible message fragments. An incorrect 'e' instead of 'l' in 'land' in target sentence (V C), for instance, may upon a closer inspection turn out to be intended as the initial letter of the phrase 'et skip' ('a ship'). What in earlier psycholinguistic inquiries of the guessing-game type has been assessed as errors per position and measures of redundancy is thus clearly the end product of a subtle interplay of presuppositions and anticipatory comprehension, and hence evidence of a very composite and complex *communicative competence*. The computer's statistical knowledge, on the other hand, is achieved at the cost of contextual sensitivity, and in that respect on a par with data on sequential constraints based upon pooled human guessing performances across a variety of different target sentences. Its strategy is in fact loaded with a confounding of all intralinguistic contexts on which its conditional probabilities are based. And it remains totally ignorant of those spatial–temporal–interpersonal coordinates of the entire act which, even though at first only vaguely and adventurously inferred, provide his human competitor with a successively more reliable basis for anticipatory comprehension.

We have dwelt with human performance in the guessing game at such length because it provides us with evidence by which we can compare a hermeneutic approach to anticipatory comprehension with that of psycholinguistic application of information theory and, by rejecting either of them, prepare the ground for a third alternative. A confrontation between programmatically presented hermeneutics and early advocates of information theory within psycholinguistics provides us with a picture of the cleavage between traditional humanities and modern social sciences at its worst, and we are actually in such a situation offered little more than a choice between *empirically inaccessible spiritualities* on the one hand and fictitious, even though *measurable, trivialities* on the other. The activity by which something is made known by verbal means in particular situations can neither be properly assessed in terms of free-floating 'potentialities of human existence' (see p. 89) nor in terms of internalized statistical knowledge of sequential constraints upon sounds of speech or strings of letters.

Some of the basic ideas of information theory, however, may as previously suggested be exploited in systematic attempts at revealing significant patterns of nesting inherent in acts of communication. Some such patterns, moreover, may involve some sort of circularity (or rather 'spirality'). We have already suggested instances of such 'spirality' such as, for instance, when some aspects of the initially unknown *here-and-now* of a target sentence, themselves anticipated or supposed on the basis of what has been made known so far, serve as a basis for anticipatory comprehension of what follows. And poorly understood aspects of the so-called hermeneutic circle may hence possibly be further illuminated in terms of observations from the guessing game.

Wellek described the hermeneutic circle of understanding as proceeding from attention to a detail to an anticipation of the whole and back again to an interpretation of the detail. Such chains of events are often reported by scholars engaged in exegesis of cryptic and incomplete texts of various kinds, and in particular in cases when the interpreter at the outset is largely ignorant with respect to authorship as well as the historical conditions under which the text came into being.

The art of interpretation represents in such a situation a task similar to that of the person engaged in our guessing game. A person guessing at (V C), for instance, may be temporarily stuck in the middle of the long compound 'Nødsignalene'. He cannot make sense at all of the sequence 'Nødsi . . .' and hits the 'g' only by resorting to an asemantic strategy. His attention is at this stage directed towards the segment 'sig . . .'. This makes him think of the word 'signal', and he immediately returns to the entire sequence 'Nødsig . . .' in order to find out whether 'signal' makes sense in the context of that whole. In doing so, he discovers to his surprise that *he has already disclosed* the word 'Nød' which, when combined with 'signal', means 'emergency'. The whole sequence is thus reinterpreted in the light of a preliminary anticipatory comprehension of a detail, and that anticipation is in turn confirmed by the reinterpretation of the whole. We have hence, in retrospect, a chain of events of precisely the kind called *a circle of understanding* by Wellek.

The detail constituting the point of departure is in such a case, as well as in many cases of exegesis of cryptic and incomplete texts, an uninterpreted segment of written discourse. This is very seldom the case in literary analysis. The detail initiating a hermeneutic circle is more often some relatively open, only partially determined, segment of a text. A careful examination of the semantic potentialities of that segment may then provide clues to tacit presuppositions on the part of the author and even to subtle meta-contracts and underlying ontological premises. The spiral by which increased insight is achieved may thus apparently proceed from some as yet not fully understood semantic potentiality to 'the world of the poet' and even 'the kind of silence' out of which his message is born—and then all the way back to a reinterpretation of that semantic potentiality. What has been left in silence by the creative writer and can be assessed only by prolepsis by his lay reader may hence in literary analysis become the object of reflective explication.

Kierkegaard maintained that *life is lived forward and understood backward.* This profound insight appears to be of particular relevance when we start pondering the relationship between the intuitively engaged creative writer and his competent and thoroughly reflective critic. It is evident, for instance, that the masterpieces of the Norwegian author Tarjei Vesaas were written 'forward' and intuitively, and that he left it to his critics to explicate at which level of intimacy he addressed his reader, what kind of premises were tacitly presupposed or induced, etc. And Hemingway, who obviously mastered the art of omission in theory as well as in practice, took care *not* to become reflective concerning his own work while creatively engaged in it.

He writes:

(Hemingway 1970, pp. 25–6) When I was writing, it was necessary for me to read after I had written. If you kept thinking about it, you would lose the thing that you were writing before you could go on with it next day. It was necessary to get exercise, to be tired in the body, and it was good to make love with whom you loved. That was better than anything. But afterwards, when you were empty, it was necessary to read in order not to think or worry about your work until you could do it again. I had learned already never to empty the well of my writing, but always stop while there was something there in the deep part of the well, and let it refill at night from the springs that fed it.

We have in the preceding chapter explored institutionalized aspects of language games and meta-contracts of communication, and we were in that context concerned with tacitly endorsed author-to-readers contracts as well. It was then maintained that silently and reciprocally accepted premises for intersubjectivity may become the focus of reflective consciousness under various conditions of alienation. The reverse may also hold true, however: reflective explication of an intuitively taken for granted framework for intersubjectivity may very likely lead to some sort of detachment and loss of spontaneous engagement. The intuitively engaged writer is hence afraid of reflective interference: his creativity is contingent upon intuition, and he can become a critic of his own work only when he is no longer creatively engaged in it.

The literary critic, on the other hand, has traditionally been called upon *to understand backward what has been written forward and intuitively*. He cannot, like the linguist, restrict his analysis to what is actually written only, far less constrain his theoretical efforts to models of particular segments of texts such as sentences. On the contrary: very little can be understood backward unless he expands the scope of his inquiries so as to deal with sequential structures of entire narratives and subtle 'sous-entendus' as well.

Literary analysis has thus for a long time been concerned with some of the central issues of the present work, yet—and paradoxically—with a reluctance towards reflective interference at times nearly equal to that of the creative writer intuitively engaged in his work. 'Moments of understanding' within the art of interpretation may possibly be ruined by interference from theories developed within neighbouring fields. The hermeneutic scholar's reserved attitude towards social scientific quantification of irrelevancies is indeed justified, and so is his scepticism towards an increasingly formalistic linguistics. His own 'moments of understanding', however, resemble transient islands of intuition in a universe of heterogeneous, though reflectively assessed, fragments of knowledge: they seem to emerge out of a trade whose theoretical foundation—while uncontaminated by linguistics and modern social science—remains largely unexplored.

But that need not be the case forever. Our inquiries into the architecture of intersubjectivity were indeed conducted with a confessed disregard for academic barriers, and with a firm intention to steer clear of the Scylla of inaccessible spiritualities as well as the Charybdis of measurable trivialities and irrelevancies. We have tried to explore general aspects of verbal communication, moreover, showing how the basic premises for intersubjectivity remain the same across a variety of different language games. What we have found out about pre-established and actively induced presuppositions, nesting patterns and anticipatory comprehension may hence be conceived of as fragments of a general and comprehensive conceptual framework, in principle equally applicable in literary analysis and in attempts at assessing what is made known in particular cases of everyday conversation. Our final task will be to bring together what we have found into a coherent analysis of message structure.

V. 2. Message Structure and Message Potential

The preceding section aimed primarily at an exploration of *the activity* by which something is made known. Human discourse has its basis in some pre-established social reality, and it is a genuinely social activity extending over real time. *What* is made known to me in any particular act of verbal communication is hence hardly ever entirely novel, but comprehensible only when bound to something I knew or assumed to be the case already. It can for that reason only be fully assessed 'backward'.

We have earlier, in our critique of transformational grammar and generative semantics, tried to reveal the futility of assessing deep sentence structures for utterances *in vacuo* and the fallacy of assigning propositional content to semantic potentialities. Deep sentence structure and propositional content represent abstractions in which language has been deprived not only of its temporal dimension, but also of its connection with the pre-established social reality. Message structure, on the other hand, will in part be assessed as a sequential structure by which semantic potentialities inherent in what is said (and hence shared perspectives and categorizations) are nested on to particular entities and aspects of a temporarily shared social world.

We have already examined a number of cases of such nesting, showing how what is made known at one particular stage constitutes part of a shared social reality and serves as a basis for anticipatory comprehension at subsequent stages. Our inquiries were then, however, obviously aimed at temporal or quasi-temporal aspects of the process of comprehension. Let us therefore now return to one such particular case and try to show *how assessment of message structure differs from an analysis of propositional content.* Consider, once more, the situation at the entrance of the apartment house and the utterance.

(V B) The old man is poor (see p. 93).

I have tried to show elsewhere how Chomsky's initial explications of deep sentence structures were confounded by propositional analysis (see Rommetveit 1972 a, b). His *ad hoc* illustrations were in part attempts at dissolving composite sentences (*in vacuo*) into sets of underlying simple assertions from which their surface structures could be derived (see, for instance, Chomsky

1965, pp. 22 and 70). By extrapolation from Chomsky's early examples we may hence dissolve (V B) into the two constituent assertions

(V C) The man is poor;

and

(V D) The man is old.

The very same assertions, moreover, would appear in sentences such as

(V E) The man is old and poor;

and

(V F) The poor man is old.

It goes without saying that such an approach implies assigning propositional content to only partially determined semantic potentialities. The very plausible 'pitying aspect' of 'poor' in (V F), for instance, must be disregarded, and a continuation such as '*He doesn't know what to do with all his money*' is hence prohibited.

Such attempts at dissolving a sentence into a set of constituent propositional statements from which it can be derived, however, are in perfect agreement with traditional linguistic conceptions of presuppositions as assertions that remain unquestioned across negation. We may, for instance, deny what is supposed to be maintained in (V B) by saying

(V G) The old man is not poor.

Since the scope of negation in this case is 'poor' only, we may in accordance with such a traditional notion of presupposition argue that (VD), or rather the assertion

(V H) There exists a man who is old,

is left unchanged.

The transformation of the segment 'The old man' in (V B) into the quasi-propositional form (V D) and further into (V H), however, implies assumptions concerning usage which are definitely false in view of our previous analysis of the nesting pattern involved in the utterance when embedded in the new tenant setting. Propositions as defined within traditional two-valued propositional logic are statements that can be assigned unequivocal truth values, and it is quite clear that 'The old man' can neither be questioned nor proved true or false in the same way as 'is poor'. It serves its function in the (potentially assertive) act of communication if and only if the two participants tag it on to the same person in a shared social world, and it fails if the speaker has one particular person X in mind whereas the listener is thinking of some other person Y. The fact that X and Y both happen to be *old men* does not help at all on such an occasion. Nor does it help that (V H), as an autonomous existential statement detached from (V B), is accepted as true by both participants in the act of communication.

What is entirely lost in the preceding analysis of propositional content is thus a crucial distinction between what is being assumed as a pre-established social reality and what is being made known, i.e. the distinction between *free* as opposed to *bound* information. This distinction was in our earlier analysis of nesting patterns introduced as an abstract and dequantified descendant from the logic of information theory, and it will be of central importance in our subsequent analysis of message structure.

The fragment 'The . . . man' in (V B) is, when uttered in the new tenant setting, first of all *free* or *unconditionally taken for granted* in the sense that it conveys information that is not supposed to be questioned at all. The particular person referred to represents presumably an inhabitant of the intersubjectively established *here-and-now* at the moment of the act of speech. He is in-tended—and presupposed as intended—to be known already.

The word 'old' is bound to 'The . . . man' in the sense that what is made known by it can only be transmitted on the assumption that it is said about 'the . . . man'. The distinction is thus a distinction between entities which are asymmetrically related, and the relationship between them is *an abstract relation of dependency*. It is hence analogous to that between *free* and *bound morphemes* in words such as 'planes' and 'explains': the free morpheme ('plane' and 'explain') is in neither case dependent upon identification of the bound morpheme in order to be interpreted. The bound morpheme, on the other hand, is in either case dependent upon the free. Indeed, the very semantic identity of the final 's' is in the present case dependent upon whether it is bound to 'plane' or to 'explain'.

We shall in our analysis of message structure, however, use the notions of '*free*' versus '*bound*' in an abstract and relative sense. The fragment 'The . . . man' conveys in the particular setting we have described information that is *free* relative to whatever is conveyed by the remaining part of the utterance in that setting. It may hence be said to constitute part of the premises for the game, i.e. a pre-condition for making known (or asserting) whatever the speaker intends to make known by 'is poor'. Such premises may fail, though, and the listener may in that case ask 'Whom are you talking about?'. The speaker will then realize that his tacitly proposed contract has *not* been endorsed by the listener. Since 'The . . . man' obviously in that case cannot be taken for granted, it must accordingly itself be *bound* to other potentially shared aspects of their social worlds.

Also, the word 'old', once *bound* to '*The . . . man*' on the premises of the speaker, represents part of the free information to which 'is poor' is bound. This implies simply that the old age of the particular person the two neighbours have in mind is taken for granted by both of them, as if by a tacit contract.[7] The speaker is, as we have shown, in control of the *here-and-now*: it is up to *him* to propose what is to be taken for granted. The listener may of course question it, saying 'But he is not old'. What he then is denying, however, is *not* what the speaker intended to make known, but part of his tacitly proposed premises.

Such tacitly proposed premises can clearly not be assessed for sentences *in vacuo*. The early practice of dissolving surface structures into underlying constituent assertions may hence in retrospect, when evaluated on the basis of recent modifications of the Harvard–M.I.T. approach, most plausibly be conceived of as preliminary attempts at revealing what can potentially be asserted or made known. The dissolution of (V B) into (V C) and (V D) should accordingly not be interpreted as an analysis of propositional content, but rather as a preliminary procedure for revealing *message potential.* And the full message potential of a given sentence, moreover, might be conceived of as *the entire set of assertions that can be mediated by that sentence within a certain range of plausible communication settings.*[8]

The full message potential of (V B) is obviously *not* assessed by dissolving it into (V C) and (V D). Additional potential assertions are brought to our attention as soon as we start pondering what may be conveyed by intonational variants of the sentence in response to different questions. In accordance with Chomsky's revised programme for explicating semantic interpretations (see p. 15) we may, for instance, examine what is being asserted in a situation in which 'man' is emphasized in response to a question *whether it is the old woman or the old man who is poor.* We may also imagine settings when 'is' is being stressed in response to uncertainty *whether the man's poverty pertains to his past only.* Chomsky's analysis of focus and presupposition in such cases may indeed be interpreted as a general formula for assessing what is presented as *novel information* as opposed to *what is already assumed to be the case.* It may thus be explored as a possible procedure for assessing message potential in accordance with the notions of *bound* and *free information* as indicated above.

Chomsky's revised programme, however, represents in its initial and incomplete form little more than a sketch of a procedure by which an analysis of propositional content of a sentence *in vacuo* can be expanded to contexts generated by extrapolation from that sentence. The focus of the sentence is a phrase containing its intonation centre, and the presupposition is an expression derived by replacing the focus by a variable. It is quite clear, moreover, that Chomsky conceives of the focus as an autonomously assessed entity, by no means bound to either remaining parts of what is actually said or to tacitly and reciprocally endorsed presuppositions. He writes:

(Chomsky 1972, footnote p. 101) . . . the focus must be composed of *full lexical items*—more generally, items that make a contribution to the meaning of a sentence that is in some sense *independent of anything outside the focus.* (Italics mine)

Such a claim of independence is legitimate within formal propositional analysis—indeed, as legitimate as the request for invariance of semantic elements across different contexts (see p. 17). It goes contrary to nesting patterns encountered in message transmission in everyday life, however, and is definitely false in view of our analysis of message structure in connection with (V B) in the new tenant setting. The focus is in that case 'poor' (or 'is poor'), and the pattern of intonation is precisely the same as when (V B) is uttered in front of a bad piece of work by an aged painter. Very different procedures are required in order to verify what is asserted on those two occasions, however. And what is made known or asserted by 'poor' can in neither case be fully assessed until we are able to relate *what is said* in a systematic fashion to *what in each situation is tacitly and reciprocally presupposed.*

We have in Chapter IV.1 tried to show how this can be achieved if we conceive of whole utterances or even longer segments of discourse as bound by tacitly endorsed contracts: 'les sous-entendus' of (V B) in the new tenant setting are such that what is said about poverty—by veridical anticipatory comprehension—is immediately understood in terms of *insufficiency with respect to financial resources*. The conversation in front of the inferior painting, on the other hand, is bound by a tacitly induced joint commitment by which 'poor' is spontaneously intended and understood in terms of *talents or skill*. A complete explication of message structure must for that reason transcend what is said. In order to identify and interpret what Chomsky claims to assess independently, as constituting 'the focus', we have in the present case even to explore tacitly endorsed meta-contracts of communication.

His 'full lexical item'—in the present case the word 'poor'—is certainly a free morpheme to which, for example, a suffix such as '. . . er' or '. . . est' may be bound, yet in itself only partially determined. *It constitutes a set of related semantic potentialities, each of which represents a potential contract by which shared categorization may be achieved.* Agreement with respect to which such potentiality is intended may accordingly also be pre-established by meta-communication. I may for instance say, at a certain stage of a dialogue, 'I am now going to talk about poverty in terms of lack of property and low income'. Or I may say 'Let us now agree to voice our frank opinions of that old painter with respect to his artistic performance'. Listening on *my* premises to a subsequent utterance such as (V B) implies different commitments on those two occasions, commitments which in the two situations described above clearly have been tacitly endorsed.

The message structure of (V B) in the new tenant setting may hence be tentatively described in terms of a composite pattern of nesting of bound to free information. What is made known by the entire utterance (and accordingly also by the presumedly focal word 'poor') is bound by a tacitly endorsed meta-contract, formally similar to what generative grammarians have called 'a selection restriction'. 'The . . . man' is bound to some already experientially identified entity within the intersubjectively established *here-and-now* of the act of speech, and '*old*' is via 'The . . . man' bound to some particular aspect of a pre-established shared social world, temporarily introduced into that shared *here-and-now*. What is conveyed by 'is poor', finally, is bound to 'The old man' and by the tacitly endorsed meta-contract.

Comprehending what is made known by (V B) in that particular situation may accordingly be conceived of as solving a complex equation: what is initially unknown to the listener can only become known to him when tagged on to his pre-established social world by a sequence of intermediary and interdependent operations. He must know, first of all, *which kind of game is going on*. He must know (or rather, take for granted) that he is engaged in discourse about real states of affairs as opposed to, for example, some imaginary world of a creative writer. It must be taken for granted, moreover, that those real states of affairs have to do with matters of money rather than, for example, with artistic achievements. 'The . . . man' has to be experientially identified as presupposed by the speaker, and his old age taken for granted—or, at least, not objected to in such a way that his intersubjectively established identity is endangered. These are prerequisites for deciding *what* is made known by the focal phrase 'is poor'—and hence also for deciding which real states of affairs have to be looked into in order to find out whether it is true.

Our inquiries into the foundations of intersubjectivity led to the general conclusion that intersubjectivity in some sense has to be taken for granted in order to be achieved. This is further corroborated in a careful analysis of message structure once we venture to go beyond a traditional semantic analysis of what is said and into a detailed analysis of tacit presuppositions as well. All prerequisites we have revealed in the particular case above may thus be conceived of as manifestations of a basic, reciprocally accepted and in some sense self-fulfilling presupposition concerning complementarity. The latter is not only revealed in presuppositions concerning a temporarily shared social world, but also in reciprocal faith in a common code of general semantic potentialities by which an expanded commonality with respect to perspectives and categorizations can be achieved.

We started our exploration of message structure by relating it to early attempts at assessing propositional content for sentences *in vacuo*. Linguists and psycholinguists engaged in such attempts were clearly influenced by Chomsky's initial programme for syntactic analysis (Chomsky 1957), but also by propositional analysis as developed within formal logic. This was occasionally revealed in terms such as 'logical subject', 'logical predicate' and even 'logical object', and I have tried to show elsewhere (Rommetveit 1968a, p. 112a, 1972a, b) how such a terminology grew out of a confounding of formal logic, generative syntax and categorical grammar.

As a next step, we tried to relate our distinction between bound and free information to Chomsky's revised scheme for semantic interpretation. His attempt at identifying the focus of an utterance was tentatively interpreted as aiming at an assessment of what is novel and initially unknown, as opposed to that which is already assumed to be the case, or, possibly, of what is asserted as distinguished from pre-conditions for asserting. The term 'focus' may hence be conceived of as a presumedly linguistically defined replacement of the somewhat awkward 'logical predicate': it is linguistically defined since it is supposed to be composed of full lexical items and can be assessed only with reference to the intonation centre of the utterance, yet—in accordance with criteria borrowed from the logic of predication—assumed to be independent of either verbally expressed or tacit presuppositions.

Our analysis of message structure aims at transcendence of such a narrowly defined linguistic perspective. The logic of predication constitutes a very complex and still not yet fully explored field. The requirement that the predicate of a proposition must be assessed independently can hardly be dissociated from the request for unequivocal truth values for composite propositional statements. It must hence be conceived of as part of the axiomatic basis for traditional logical analysis. Wittgenstein referred to predication, however, as 'a form complete in itself' (Wittgenstein 1961, p. 18); whereas Weinreich (1963, p. 119) conceived of it as a general semiotic form.

Issues of predication are thus, when considered so broadly, familiar. They have been explored throughout this work, but inductively, and in connection with case studies of language in action. And our persistent inquiries into what is made known by particular acts of verbal communication have by now made it perfectly clear that novelty by no means implies independence, either from verbally induced or tacitly endorsed presuppositions. On the contrary: what would correspond to the predicate in a propositional analysis of a given utterance appears to be bound in subtle ways to other segments of that utterance as well as to particular silently endorsed premises.

The classical dichotomy of argument *versus* predicate from formal logic is for that reason of restricted value if it is our aim to understand rather than prescribe or pass judgment on ordinary language in action. Our approach therefore also represents a deliberate deviation from traditional analysis of predication, and is one in which traditional logic of predication has been modified in accordance with the logic of information theory. Analysis of message structure will hence have a dual aim: we shall not only try to distinguish what is novel from that which is presupposed, but also attempt to reveal how whatever is made known by verbal means is bound to a temporarily shared social world. Even intralinguistic structures may then be considered ramifications of the same basic architecture of intersubjectivity and thus, in some important respects, on a par with tacitly endorsed premises.

This has already been indicated in connection with utterance (V B) in the new tenant setting: the opening phrase 'The old man' may in some other setting be replaced by 'He', and what is made known (and possibly asserted) by the entire utterance may indeed under still other conditions be achieved by the cryptic and elliptic remark 'Poor'. Linguistically mediated free information can thus in principle under conditions of a more perfectly temporarily shared social world be replaced by extralinguistically induced presuppositions. What is obtained by tacitly endorsed meta-contracts, moreover, can under conditions of less perfect pre-established premises for inter-subjectivity only be achieved by explicit meta-communication.

Such functional equivalence, once properly recognized, has also important implications for assessment of *what* is made known or asserted in particular cases. Consider, for instance, some possible intonational variants of (V B) in response to different questions. The word 'man' may thus on one occasion be stressed in response to the question 'Is it the old *man* or the old *woman* who is poor?'. The issue is on another occasion whether it is the *old* man or the *young* man who is poor, and 'old' is consequently stressed in the response.

The question may in such situations actually be entirely superfluous, and it serves in the present context only to make explicit what is presupposed: it is in either case taken for granted that *only one out of two already intersubjectively identified persons is poor*. The only significant difference between the two situations pertains to the temporarily shared social world at the moment of speech: what Ducrot (1972, p. 242) has coined the 'exhibited universe' (*'univers montré'*) consists in the one case of two particular persons, one of which is an old man and the other an old woman, whereas in the other case it consists of that same old man and one particular young man. The whole phrase 'The old man' serves in either case to point out one and only one particular and already fully identified person, moreover, and this holds true whether 'old' or 'man' is stressed. What is made known by the word constituting the intonational centre of the response in each case is hence neither *age* nor *sex* as such, but rather *who is poor*. The full contribution of the stressed word can thus be properly assessed if and only if we explore the pattern of dependency involved and keep in mind how the entire phrase within which it is contained is bound to some particular and already tacitly identified entity within the temporarily shared social world.

Let us therefore compare what is made known by the stressed *'man'* in the case above with what is achieved by the very same stressed word under—apparently—only slightly divergent conditions. Imagine a dialogue, for instance, in which both participants believe beforehand (and know that the other believes as well) that some old person in their neighbourhood is living on relief money. None of them has any idea concerning *who* that person might be, however. One of the participants in the dialogue does not even know whether the person living on relief is *a woman* or *a man*. Precisely that seems to be made known to him, however, as the other says

(V I) An old *man* is poor.

We might be tempted to conclude—in accordance with Chomsky's definition of the focus as autonomous and composed of full lexical items—that what is made known or asserted in this particular case includes at least the entire *'man'*. And that implies in turn, if we also adopt the Harvard–M.I.T. approach of decomposing lexical items into invariant semantic features, at least the features *'human'*, *'male'* and *'adult'*.

However, the silent premises on which (V I) is said and understood are evidently such as, for example,

(V J) There exists in the neighbourhood an old human being who is poor,

and 'old' implies, of course, adulthood. *What is made known is thus not at all the entire 'man', but rather what is left of its meaning potential when species and age aspects have been subtracted.* It may accordingly even be described in terms of information theory, as reduction of an initial state of uncertainty: the listener's ignorance with respect to the identity of the person mentioned in (V I) is reduced from a state of uncertainty corresponding to the whole set of old human beings in the neighbourhood to a proper subset consisting of all males only.

If anyone should happen to question what is asserted in (V I) and wants to disprove it on empirical grounds, he would thus obviously restrict his investigations in the neighbourhood to old human beings only. Let us imagine that the listener actually conducts such an investigation, and that it then turns out that there is in fact no single old man living on relief. He may then argue that what has been asserted by his partner in the dialogue is false. The latter may in turn send him back to investigate all old women as well, however, and it may turn out that there is no single woman living on relief either. What has been disproved in that case is hence *not* the assertion he set out to test, but rather *the jointly endorsed premises for asserting (V I)*.

An analysis of message structure has thus revealed significant differences with respect to what is made known by the stressed '*man*' in the two cases, i.e. in (V B) as opposed to (V I). The word is in the first case via the definite article '*The* . . .' bound to an entity which has already been intersubjectively identified in the THAT region of the temporarily shared social world (see Figure 1, p. 36). The whole phrase within which it is contained is for that reason analogous to a pointing gesture. What is made known by '*man*' in (V I), on the other hand, is one additional characteristic (sex) of an entity that has been presupposed, but so far only partially determined. And the difference with respect to what is asserted is further corroborated by a careful examination of relevant and plausible verification procedures in the two cases. We find, then, that what would correspond most closely to the predicate in a formal propositional analysis is neither autonomous nor composed of full lexical items. It has in each case to be revealed by a thorough analysis of the ways in which apparently novel and previously unknown segments of what is said are bound to whatever in each particular situation has been jointly and tacitly presupposed.

In order to spell out the message structure revealed by such analysis we have at times resorted to more rigidly defined information theory, formal propositional analysis, and even semantic analysis of the Harvard–M.I.T. brand. The reader may for that reason be left with the suspicion that we shall finally seek safety in some sort of (eclectic) formalistic escapism, despite solemn promises to the contrary. Let us therefore at this stage turn to acts of verbal communication whose message structure cannot be assessed at all by such already available formal devices and, more specifically, to language use that has even been relegated as anomalous or ungrammatical on formal grounds.

We have in Chapter II discussed a number of such cases, but at that stage without presenting any explicitly elaborated alternative to the Harvard–M.I.T. approach. It is quite clear, however, that many of the so-called anomalies so eagerly exhibited by semanticists of the Harvard–M.I.T. at an early stage make perfect sense once we add some plausible context. Consider, for instance, once more:

(V K) My spinster aunt is an infant.

It is possible to conceive of an almost infinite number of plausible settings for such a sentence by varying extralinguistic conditions and the I–you coordinate of the act of communication. We may, first of all, consider real-life settings in which the speaker is talking about a particular aunt of his. What is made known will then, of course, depend upon what at the moment of speech has been tacitly presupposed. Such presuppositions, moreover, may be brought to the foreground by surveying plausible questions to which (V K) may provide the answer. These may concern, for example, *how* the speaker's spinster aunt is, what he thinks of her, *which* of his aunts is an infant, *who* is an infant, etc.

We may also consider entirely different settings. (V K) may thus be the opening sentence in a poem or a novel. And it may even occur as an instance of meta-language in a discussion between two linguists. One of them may, for instance, want to make known to the other how the word 'infant' can be used in ways the latter has not yet considered. He may then by (V K) try to persuade his opponent—an orthodox semanticist of the Harvard–M.I.T. school—that the word contains within its rich meaning potential an abstract, yet not fully identified, feature of innocent dependence, a feature he feels is personified in his spinster aunt.

Let us now briefly consider only a few such contextual variants, and start with the real-life situation when 'an infant' in (V K) is stressed in response to a question concerning *how* the speaker's spinster aunt is. Let us assume, moreover, that the listener already knows that lady by sight. The message structure of (V K) is under such conditions very similar to that of (V B) in the new tenant setting (see p. 101): what is made known by 'an infant' is bound to 'My spinster aunt', and the latter is in turn bound to an already intersubjectively identified entity within the temporarily shared social world at the moment of the act of speech. What is intended by the speaker and presupposed to be intended by him on the part of his listener is hence neither, for example, *incapacity to speak*[9] nor *early stage within the life cycle*, but rather some abstract and only partially determined potentiality such as immaturity or the one proposed in the imaginary meta-linguistic discussion referred to above.

Let us, next, examine a case when (V K) is uttered in response to *who* is an infant. The latter question may for instance be raised in an informal and noisy discussion about candidates for political offices, one of whom happens to be the spinster aunt. The conversation in such a situation is by a tacitly endorsed meta-contract restricted to adult persons only. What is said about them, moreover, is bound by a commitment to a shared perspective: it has to do with their potential capacities as *politicians* rather than with the persons as, for instance, *artists* or *athletes*.

Even an overheard fragment of an utterance such as '. . . *is an infant*' is for that reason immediately understood in terms of the general abstract potentiality suggested above, but on this occasion constrained by 'le sous-entendu' that the unknown person is claimed to be an infant when viewed as a politician. And (V K) uttered in response to the question '*Who* is an infant?' is hence, by anticipatory comprehension, 'perfectly understood': *it makes known whom the speaker declares immature with respect to political insight and skill.*

Which semantic potentialities of '*an infant*' are intended and understood as intended can thus only be revealed by assessing the message structure in each particular case. We have therefore, first of all, to examine how the phrase is bound to other segments of the utterance and to tacitly endorsed presuppositions. Its entire set of semantic potentialities must subsequently be matched against all presuppositions to which the phrase is bound, and we have to examine *if* and eventually *how* what is already taken for granted overlaps with what otherwise (in other contexts) might be made known by the expression.

We find, then, that some potentialities have to be disregarded on the grounds that what would be made known by them is *already presupposed*. This was the case with species and age potentialities of '*man*' in (V I), and it is also true of, for example, a semantic potentiality such as *animate* of the phrase '*an infant*' in all the cases we have analysed above.[10]

Other semantic potentialities are *overruled* by what in that particular act of communication is taken for granted. This applies to *age* or *stage of life cycle* potentialities of 'an infant' in all cases we have discussed: stage of life cycle is unequivocally conveyed by 'spinster' and constitutes part of the unquestioned, free information to which 'an infant' is bound. This, of course, also holds true for (V K) in the setting in which it appears as the opening sentence of a novel, and when it represents an instance of meta-language. And such overruling is by no means an arbitrary or magical affair: the outcome is strictly determined by nesting of bound to free information, and the phenomenon as such has for ages been explored in literary analysis of metaphors.

An elimination of redundant and overruled semantic potentialities, how-ever, yields only a partial determination of what is made known. We have thus so far, in the case of the expression 'an infant', only restricted what is made known to a subset of its semantic potentialities defined by the elimination of *animate* and *early stage of life cycle*. What is left may therefore perhaps plausibly be described in terms of abstract, but largely open potentialities such as, for example, *innocent dependency* and *immaturity*. And such a description may in fact represent a very plausible account of what is achieved by the expression when (V K) appears in the novel: the reader may not be supposed to be any more fully informed at all at that stage, since the innocent dependency and/or immaturity of that spinster aunt is possibly going to be a central theme as he continues reading.

What is left open and largely undetermined after our procedure of elimina-tion, however, may in other cases be further specified in view of additional presuppositions to which the expression is bound. This is clearly the case in the noisy and informal discussion of political candidates: whatever is made known by 'an infant' when said about some such candidate is by a tacit meta-contract bound to refer to him in his capacity as a politician. This does not by any means imply that the expression has been fully and finally determined. On the contrary: the remark may very likely initiate a lengthy dialogue concerning what, more precisely, has been asserted by 'an infant'. What has been 'perfectly understood', however, is that neither status as animate nor stage of life cycle nor immaturity in general has been asserted. Further specification may hence safely be constrained to an explication of, *political immaturity* and, possibly, of *semantically mediated emotive and attitudinal contagion*.

This is indeed a deplorably poor achievement when gauged against criteria developed within formal logic, yet not so poor when we keep in mind that it is achieved *in* and *about* a multifaceted, only partially shared, and only fragmentarily known world. Even such a partial determination of what is made known is in certain respects quite an impressive performance, definitely beyond the capacity of a person in a schizophrenic or autistic state of mind and, we shall argue, also beyond what can be accounted for by the expanded versions of propositional analysis proposed by linguists of the Harvard–M.I.T. school. It presupposes complementarity and reciprocal taking the role of the other: the speaker must monitor what he says on the premises of the listener, and the latter must listen on those of the speaker. Both of them, moreover, must continually relate what is said at any particular stage of their dialogue to whatever at that stage has been jointly presupposed.

What at times is said and 'perfectly understood' in a real-life situation may for that reason appear blatantly anomalous and utterly incomprehensible *in vacuo*, when nothing is known about tacit presuppositions to which it is bound. Consider, for instance, the following excerpt from a dialogue:

(V L) He was bigger when he was smaller, and he will become bigger when he gets big, because his father was also small when he was smaller.

The passage is a literal translation of part of an anecdote and—at least in its Norwegian version—perfectly comprehensible in the particular setting of that anecdote. A mother is walking with her four-year-old son in the road. She meets another lady who, knowing that the boy is four years old, says:

(V M) Your son is small to be that age.

The excerpt above is then uttered in response to (V M), and the clue by which it becomes comprehensible has thus actually been provided by the lady to whom it is addressed: she has by (V M) initiated a dialogue about *body size as related to age*, and what is said in response to (V M) by the mother is bound to that presupposition.

This implies, more specifically, that each clause is intended and, by anticipatory comprehension, understood as making known something about bodily size as related to age. The latter of the two adjectives in the clause—even though in each case some variant of either 'big' or 'small'—must hence always be understood as making known aspects of age. Its otherwise by far salient semantic potentiality, size, is immediately disregarded on the basis of what is tacitly presupposed. And what is made known (and possibly asserted) can accordingly be rephrased as,

(V N) He was—as far as ratio of age to size is concerned—bigger when he was younger, and he will get bigger—again, relatively speaking—when he reaches adulthood, because his father was also small for his age when *he* was younger.

Apparent anomalies such as (V K) and (V L) were once with great care and enthusiasm 'proved' anomalous by semanticists of the Harvard–M.I.T. school (see, for instance, Katz and Fodor 1963). Such 'proofs' were produced by assigning propositional form and content to sentences *in vacuo*. They are accordingly in retrospect, and even when viewed from the perspective of the expanded Harvard–M.I.T. approach, evidence of a total disregard for the interplay of tacit presuppositions and semantic potentialities in acts of verbal communication.

We have tried to show, however, how the practice of assigning propositional content to semantic potentialities reappears in the various revised and expanded versions as well, including, as we have seen, Chomsky's own revised scheme for semantic interpretations. It thus seems to pervade all ramifications like a hereditary sin, apparently rooted in a notion of predication different from that on which our analysis of message structure is based. This is revealed in Chomsky's definition of the focus of a sentence as independent and composed of full lexical items, and also in his attempts at accounting for general semantic potentialities in terms of underlying propositional form. He maintains about what is made known by the adjectives 'easy' and 'difficult', for instance:

> (Chomsky 1972, p. 23) ... easy (difficult) appears in base phrasemarkers as an adjective predicated of propositions as subject ((for us) to please John is easy, etc.); forms such as it is easy (for us) to please John are derived by extraposition.

It is *not* easy (for me) to decide what is meant, more precisely, either by 'predicated of' or by 'propositions' in the quotation above. If we consider what *can be made known* by an utterance such as

(V O) John is easy to please

when embedded in variant communication settings, we are immediately faced with a whole range of possibilities. Every single content element may in principle become the focus of message transmission, depending upon what is already assumed to be the case. The sentence may accordingly serve to make known *who* is easy to please; whether John (who used to be) no longer *is* easy to please; whether John is difficult or *easy* to please; or *in what respect* John is easy. We have, in addition, to take into consideration possible combinations of content elements such as, for instance, '*easy to please*' in response to *how John is* and '*John . . . to please*' in response to *what is easy*.

Chomsky's claim that '*easy* ... appears in base phrasemarkers as an adjective predicated of propositions' is clearly *not* concerned with what is made known or asserted as opposed to what is taken for granted in particular settings such as those suggested above. His aim is rather to reveal features that remain invariant across all of them, and one such feature appears to be a tacit presupposition: adjectives such as '*easy*' and '*difficult*' are such that some task is presupposed whenever the adjective is employed. The task taken for granted in all contextual variants of (V O) may thus be expressed as, for example, *(for us) to please John*.

Chomsky offers no reason why the latter expression should be considered a proposition. However, a proposition is by definition—unlike a task—an entity to which an unequivocal truth value can be assigned. What is achieved by rebaptizing tasks as 'propositions' is hence hardly any more 'deep' understanding of what invariably is made known by sentences such as (V O), but rather an arbitrarily introduced and fictitious basis for assessment of abstract propositional content. Truth values of such sentences should, according to Chomsky's analysis of deep structure, be revealed by a stepwise procedure: we have first to determine what is made known by '(for us) to please John' in order to assess what is claimed to be true in (V O).

This implies, in turn, that sentences such as, for example,

(V P) John is easy

are undetermined as far as propositional content is concerned, i.e. (V P) must be considered an incomplete version of, for example, (V O). And we may argue, following Chomsky, that the same holds true for pairs of sentences such as

(V Q) Mathematics is difficult

and

(V R) Mathematics is difficult to teach.

This leads us back to the general issue of partial determination of expressions, however. We may accordingly add other instances of relative incompletion such as, for instance,

(V S) John is eager

versus

(V S$_e$) John is eager to start

versus

(V S$_{ee}$) John is eager to start teaching.

And (V P), moreover, while considered a possible completion of what is made known by (V O), is in itself clearly only *partially determined* when compared to a possible and plausible expansion such as, for example,

(V P$_e$) John is easy to please as far as food is concerned.

The dichotomy between propositions on the one hand and undetermined expressions on the other is in view of such examples clearly a fictitious dichotomy. And the lesson to be learned is simple, yet of crucial theoretical significance: the issue of partial determination of expressions within natural language cannot be solved by formalistic escapisms such as, for example, labelling tasks 'propositions', but has to be dealt with in terms of nesting of bound to free information. Nothing can be asserted *in vacuo*, and hardly anything can be achieved by gauging what is conveyed by a word such as 'easy' against abstractions presumedly borrowed from formal logic. We have on an earlier occasion, however, tried to examine what is intended and understood by the word in terms of a verbally induced contract concerning cognitive categorization (see p. 26).

What is implied by such a shared perspective, however, cannot be fully understood unless we also examine alternative, though interdependent, cognitive categorizations. Our inquiries must hence be expanded: it is not sufficient to investigate purely intralinguistic relationships; what is tacitly presupposed must ultimately also be described in terms of decentered cognition of human action and personal causality. And these are issues that have been systematically explored by Michotte (1954) and, quite extensively, by Heider in his 'naive analysis of action'. Heider maintains, for instance, concerning the relationship between attributing ease to tasks and ability to persons:

(Heider 1958, p. 99) Thus, if a task is easy, or if a person has good ability, then we expect the person to be able to engage successfully in the action. Or, if we know that

p lacks the necessary powers to do something, such as ability or endurance, then we shall not expect him to do it.
(p. 111) . . . if two people exert themselves to the same degree, the one who solves the more difficult task has the greatest power. The one who has to exert himself more to solve a task of a given difficulty has the lesser power. And the greatest power or ability will be shown by the person who solves a difficult task with little exertion.

What is conveyed by words such as 'easy' can therefore, in view of Heider's penetrating analysis of attribution, only be understood if we venture to inquire into a whole repertoire of intimately related categorizations. Actions may under certain conditions be conceived of as *tasks*; a *try* is required in order to assess whether the person trying to do something *can* do it;[11] *success* may be attributed to *ease* of tasks or *ability* of persons performing them, or both, etc. Inherent in such a decentered scheme for cognition of human action, moreover, is a capacity for bipolar attribution: eagerness, for instance, is ordinarily attributed to persons, whereas ease and difficulty are attributed to actions or tasks.

Full mastery of such a general bipolar scheme implies that *essential residual aspects of a given composite state of affairs are in some sense taken for granted whenever one single, particular aspect is made known.* This is also in part revealed in ordinary usage when criteria of synonymy are spontaneously proposed: 'It is easy for him' is immediately understood as 'He can do it with little exertion'. What is asserted in 'He can do it', moreover, will very likely be further elaborated in an utterance such as, for example, 'He will succeed in doing it if he tries'. And what is made known by any single word such as 'easy' or 'can' is thus in such situations clearly bound to a more comprehensive scheme for categorization. The latter is for that reason analogous in some significant respects to *the square* in our dialogue on page 90; it is—even though left in silence—taken for granted as an intersubjectively shared frame of reference for making sense of what is said.

Let us pursue this analogy in somewhat more detail. We may then return to cryptic expressions such as
(V P) John is easy;
(V S) John is eager;
and also
(V T) John can.
And let us now explore each of the three expressions with respect to what is tacitly taken for granted, in principle, in the same way as we tried to assess what was tacitly presupposed at each successive stage of the question-and-answer game on page 90. What we find may then possibly be summarized as indicated in Figure 4.

Some composite state of affairs of the general form

$$[X \ (do) \ Y]$$

is evidently taken for granted in all three expressions. This general form may be

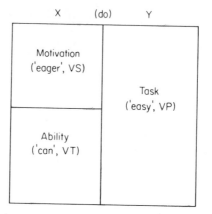

FIGURE 4. Tacit presuppositions inherent in 'easy', 'eager' and 'can'

conceived of as in some respects analogous to the entire unmentioned square in the dialogue. The two poles of the composite state of affairs, moreover, make for a subdivision analogous to that by which the square is divided into the right and the left half, since what is made known about John is dependent upon in which of two distinctively different capacities he is talked about. The word 'easy' in (V P) is thus comprehensible if and only if he is considered as part or aspect of some action or task [(do) Y]. What is conveyed by either 'eager' or 'can', on the other hand, can only be made known if John is attended to as a potential actor, i.e. as X in [X (do)]. The word 'eager', moreover, makes sense if and only if said about *motivational aspects* rather than his *ability* as a potential actor.

X and Y in the form [X (do) Y] are merely Aristotle's *agens* and *patiens* in a novel disguise. What has been added to that form by Michotte, Heider and Piaget, however, is an empirically firmly corroborated insight into phenomenal causality. Michotte and Heider were particularly concerned with the range of conditions under which adults spontaneously experience events as possessing some inherent causal structure, and their findings converge in a crucial distinction between *personal* and *impersonal causality* (see Heider 1958, p. 100). Attribution of effort and ease is thus clearly dependent upon experienced personal causality and [do (Y)] is never considered a task unless X is attended to as intentionally engaged.

Heider's inquiries into attribution are investigations of behaviourally revealed inference rules rather then explications of interrelationships between words. They may hence, like the inquiries of Levi-Strauss, be said to aim at discovery of '. . . basic structures which are common to the mental mold of the sender and the receiver of the message, and which enable a genuine intersection of the two intentionalities'. And rules for attribution are indeed some of the basic operations which enable us to transcend our initial imprisonment in a private and egocentric world. They are, in fact, also prerequisites for consensus with respect to verification: what is made known by 'John can' is proved true if he *tries* and *succeeds*.

The message potentials of expressions such as (V P), (V S) and (V T) are thus bound to a particular commonality with respect to interpretation (*'eine Interpretationsgemeinschaft'*): none of them makes sense in acts of verbal communication unless some scheme for attribution such as the one suggested in Figure 4 is tacitly presupposed and mastered by both participants in the act. Each expression is, of course, incomplete when gauged against criteria for fully determined 'propositional content', yet comprehensible and partially determined by aspects of the scheme about which nothing is said. Some task or intended action is thus always taken for granted, even though the particular nature of (do) in [X (do) Y] may remain unknown. A prerequisite for a temporarily shared social world in the case of (V P), moreover, is a capacity for decentered shifts of perspective on people such that a person can on one occasion be attended to as a source of action, and on another occasion as (an aspect of) a task.

Figure 4 may hence be said to portray *a culturally shared 'kind of silence' out of which adult discourse about ease, eagerness and ability is generated.* It can accordingly be further explored within a comparative framework, against the background of different 'kinds of silence' and as a transformation of an initially undifferentiated, egocentric and private world. We may also conceive of hypothetical alternative cultural varieties such as, on the one hand, an entirely non-manipulatory culture in which the perspective on fellow human beings tacitly presupposed in (V P) is prohibited and, on the other hand, a 'robot society' with no awareness of personal *versus* impersonal variants of causality whatsoever.

The latter distinction is in view of Michotte's and Heider's investigations a distinction between two very different modes of attribution. It is hence part and parcel of our intuitively mastered categorization of composite events and states of affairs, yet evidently ignored in recent interpretative semantics when expressions of the general form [X (do) Y] are reformulated so as to reveal some implicit causality. Let us at this stage therefore briefly reconsider Fillmore's paraphrases of KILL and PERSUADE with CAUSE (see p. 9). He writes:

> (Fillmore 1972, p. 9) The role by which KILL differs from DIE and that by which PERSUADE differs from BELIEVE is that of the individual that is 'agentively' involved in the events named by these verbs.
> Apart from this difference, we are dealing with pairs of synonyms.

It is quite clear, though, that the role of X in [X (KILL) Y] differs from that of X in [X (PERSUADE) Y]. What is made known by 'Bill PERSUADED John to believe . . .' may be paraphrased as 'Bill INTENDED, TRIED and SUCCEEDED to make John believe . . .', but neither intentionality nor effort is taken for granted in KILL. The sentence 'Peter KILLED the cat' may thus be interpreted as 'Peter CAUSE (the cat DIE)' (see Fillmore 1972, p. 4).

Whether Peter intended to do so or caused the death of the cat incidentally, however, is in that case left entirely undetermined. The strategy of attribution indicated in Figure 4 is thus tacitly presupposed in PERSUADE, but not in KILL.

'The bottom level' in our explication of message potentials is thus clearly at variance with that which emerges as deep structures in Chomsky's and Fillmore's analysis of underlying propositional form and content. And Fillmore's question (1972, p. 9) whether his reformulation of KILL and PERSUADE with CAUSE '... is indeed closer to the underlying conceptual reality' must on the basis of psychological investigations of modes of attribution be answered in the negative: the postulation of a shared and silently presupposed CAUSE serves to conceal rather than reveal what kind of contract concerning categorization is tacitly endorsed in each of the two verbs.

Fillmore's analysis of *synonymy salva veritate* deals at the bottom level with 'events named by ... verbs', however, events that may also be described in terms of scientifically established knowledge of various kinds. The feature of causation is thus taken for granted in explication of death within biology and institutionalized medicine: a certificate of death is indeed considered incomplete unless some account of the cause of death is included. The verbs DIE and KILL are hence, when mapped against such scientifically defined 'conceptual realities', synonymous apart from the role of the individual 'agentively involved' in the events. And TO DIE may accordingly—if we take Fillmore's claim concerning synonymy seriously—be paraphrased as TO BE KILLED.

Issues of life and death may be thought of and talked about from a variety of different perspectives, however, and the role of the individual 'agentively involved' in the event of dying is neither a minor nor an ontologically trivial role. What is deliberately disregarded in Fillmore's analysis of *synonymy salva veritate* may hence become the dominant semantic feature of DIE in a funeral sermon as well as in a dialogue between ordinary people in fear and anticipation of death. The role of the individual 'agentively involved' is thus made the focus of ardent intellectual inquiry in Hamlet's famous monologue:

To DIE: to sleep;
No more; and by a sleep to say we end
The Heart-ache, and the thousand natural shocks
That flesh is heir to, 'tis a consummation
Devotedly to be wish'd. To DIE, to sleep;
To sleep: perchance to dream: aye, there's the rub
For in that sleep of death what dreams may come ...

And the poetry of death is replete with similar metaphors: TO DIE is TO ENTER THE SLEEP OF DEATH, TO WITHER, TO PASS AWAY, TO RETURN TO THE SILENCE OF ETERNITY, TO FADE INTO NON-EXISTENCE.

What is conveyed by DIE in such contexts is apparently not at all bound to 'conceptual realities' defined in terms of death certificates and biological causation only. Its meaning potential has instead to be explored in terms of human conceptual and associative potentialities, i.e. as a set of potentially shared cognitive–emotive perspectives with roots in a cultural heritage consisting of myth and religion as well as of 'public' and scientifically founded biological knowledge. It is hence bound to a multifaceted and ontologically opaque commonality with respect to interpretation which—even though based upon a shared existential awareness of the inevitability of death—allows for a variety of interrelated perspectives. What is conveyed by DIE in contexts such as Hamlet's monologue is thus in part comprehensible by extrapolation from intuitively mastered modes of attribution, since *personal death may be conceived of as the final negation of intentionality and personal causality.*[12]

We have tried to show how the message potentials of particular expressions may in part be explored in terms of meaning potentials of constituent words such as, for example, POOR, INFANT, EASY, EAGER, CAN and DIE. The meaning potential of each such word, moreover, can only be assessed as a set of semantic potentialities. *And each basic semantic potentiality may in turn be conceived of as a general draft of a contract concerning categorization, ordinarily bound to some more comprehensive scheme of attribution.*

The futility of postulating 'literal meanings' thus follows from the semantic openness of ordinary language and its embeddedness in 'the stream of life': *we cannot attain closure and assess propositional content without prejudging a multifaceted, only partially known and opaque 'reality'.* Which possible perspective or categorization is intended and presupposed as intended in any particular act of communication, however, may be revealed if we examine how a particular word within that act is bound to other segments of the utterance, and how the latter in turn are bound to a temporarily shared social reality. What is made known can thus be partially determined by analysis of message structure, and the residual has in each case to be specified in terms of some unquestioned shared social reality or presupposed commonality with respect to interpretation.

The residual may in some cases be conceived of as analogous to *the axiomatic foundation for interpretation of particular scientific statements.* What is made known by EASY, EAGER and CAN in expressions such as (V P), (V S) and (V T) thus appears to be bound to a tacitly taken for granted 'space of action' in a fashion resembling that by which particular geometrically defined terms for distances, areas and volumes are bound to axiomatically defined Euclidean space.

Partial determination implies on other occasions simply *optional elaborations of some general and invariant draft of a contract.* What is conveyed by the word INFANT in a particular situation may thus be tacitly endorsed meta-contracts be intended and understood in terms of political immaturity, but such consensus may in turn serve as a point of departure for negotiations concerning specific criteria for verification. Moreover, what is made known by POOR in discourse about financial issues may be unequivocally determined in a general fashion as the opposite of WEALTHY, yet in a conversation about inhabitants of the third world be specified as, for example, *living conditions below the subsistence level* and in a dialogue about neighbours as *dependency upon public financial support*. Full mastery of the general *poverty–wealth* potentiality of POOR is thus revealed in contextually appropriate optional elaborations—and hence contingent upon the generalized capacity to adopt the perspectives of different 'others'.

The residual may in still other cases be explicated as presupposed commonality with respect to interpretation bound to some particular fragments of a cultural heritage. We speak about FALSTAFFIAN characters and DIONYSIAN styles of life, and we may try to make known our impression of particular political states of affairs by saying that they are manifestations of DE-GAULLISME. What in the dialogue between the history teacher and his African student was initially unknown and in the course of the dialogue bound to a social reality of tribal kings is thus in the latter case taken for granted as a pre-established commonality with respect to interpretation.

What is made known under conditions of intimate I–you relationships may be bound to even more restricted—and at times rather unique and experientially based—pre-conditions for communication. Kelly (1955), who in his exploration of 'personal constructs' has been particularly concerned with individual strategies of cognition in perception of self and others, reports a number of such cases. Thus, one of his patients was asked to name a particular attribute that had proved very salient in her judgment of similarities and differences between people she knew well. She then ended up with the word 'MARY-NESS': the attribute was encoded in a novel word bound to her impression of one particular friend of hers, Mary, and hence comprehensible only to people who knew and shared her impression of that particular person.

An analysis of message structure will thus—unlike assessment of propositional form and content—in every case have to deal with residuals in terms of tacitly taken for granted shared social realities and/or presupposed commonality with respect to interpretation. Such residuals, however, are *not* to be conceived of as *ad hoc* manifestations of some undifferentiated and only intuitively revealed '*Interpretationsgemeinschaft*', but must in each case be specified by a systematic analysis of nesting of bound to free information. What is claimed to be 'the real meaning' of some literary text must hence in retrospect—even if *arrived at* by 'mere intuition' and 'a circle of understanding'—in part be described in terms of pre-conditions for communication characteristic of that text. And what is conveyed by the text may then be explicated in terms of systematic interrelationships between such premises for intersubjectivity and what is actually written.

We have already briefly commented upon general premises for intersubjectivity as related to genre, arguing that certain genres of literature may be characterized in terms of emancipation from 'standard' contracts. A poetically induced *here-and-now* is thus often established by prolepsis, and the *Why* of communication may in part be described in terms of a choice between possible shared social realities. Which commonality is intended as presupposed may at times even be determined by choice between expressions that are strictly synonymous as far as 'literal meaning' is concerned. We have in Norwegian, for instance, two different words for *sheep*, namely SAU and FAAR. Only the latter is used in biblical contexts of good shepherds and lost sheep, however. FAAR may hence in a poem serve to induce a *here-and-now* of precisely such conceptual–associative potentialities—as contrasted with an equally familiar, but distinctively different social reality induced by extrapolation from the rural and secular SAU.

Cases of prolepsis in creative writing can hence in a 'backward' account of what is made known be described as particular patterns of nesting, in principle of the same kind as those by which semantic potentialities of EASY, EAGER and CAN are bound to more comprehensive schemes for attribution (see Figure 4, p. 116). And segments of a given text that are judged as entirely redundant or tautologous when examined in terms of 'literal meanings' and propositional content may be made perfectly comprehensible and even shown to be of focal significance once, after a systematic analysis of message structure, they are interpreted in the light of contextually appropriate premises. Consider, for instance, the word MAN in Kipling's poem 'If':

If you can talk with crowds and keep your virtue,
Or walk with Kings—nor lose the common touch,
If neither foes nor loving friends can hurt you,
If all men count with you, but none too much;
If you can fill the unforgiving minute
With sixty seconds' worth of distance run,
Yours is the Earth and everything that's in it,
And—which is more—you'll be a MAN, my son!

What is intended by MAN in such a context is obviously *not* a categorization in accordance with invariant 'semantic markers' such as, for example, *human, male, adult*. Such 'literal' attributes are neither contingent upon sustained virtue nor upon immunity to wounds inflicted by foes and friends, and hence clearly *overruled* by what has to be taken for granted in view of the immediately preceding text. Kipling's MAN is thus comprehensible only in terms of partially determined semantic potentialities transcending the 'literal' meaning, and whatever will be read into him will be contingent upon particular 'sous-entendus'.

We may, for instance, try to read the word as if it conveyed a focal fragment of a praise of *manhood*, addressed from father to son, and embedded in a shared social reality of male British empire-builders. In doing so, however, we have to engage in historical studies in order to be able to reconstruct and adopt particular cognitive–emotive perspectives characteristic of that historical epoch and that social reality. But we may also—irrespective of historically determined premises for intersubjectivity presupposed by the author—ponder what his message to another generation with a different cultural background may be. We may thus even try to explicate what is made known as if it were bound to an '*Interpretationsgemeinschaft*' defined in terms of current neo-feminist ideology.

A claim that the scholar has 'seized upon the *right* interpretation' of some literary text with no specification of either the tacitly assumed I–you coordinate or the residual shared social reality to which that interpretation is bound is hence a rather ambiguous claim. A *mystification of premises for intersubjectivity may be a sine qua non in exegesis of the Holy Scriptures,* provided the text is assumed to reveal divine and absolute truth: its 'real meaning' may then be conceived of as *a priori* universal, emancipated from variant human architectures of intersubjectivity, and accessible only by what hermeneutic scholars refer to as '*werkimmanente Interpretation*'. And loyalty towards 'the text as such' is warranted in interpretation of works of fiction as well, since significant premises for intersubjectivity very often are induced by prolepsis, as 'sous-entendus', rather than explicitly spelled out. Such 'sous-entendus', however, must in an analysis of message structure be specified in terms of meta-contracts and particular premises for intersubjectivity. They can be 'understood backward' if and only if their impact upon what is claimed to be 'the real meaning' of the text is explicitly spelled out. The 'I' of a work of fiction must accordingly, as Mukařovský (1971, p. 134) points out, be defined in terms of that particular work rather than the biography of the author. The world of Kipling may thus be illuminated by relevant biographical and historical investigations, yet reflectively assessed only through investigations of his writings, and in part as tacit presuppositions. The same applies to even more 'idiosyncratic' worlds such as those of Valery, Rilke and Kafka (see p. 51).

An emphasis upon the uniqueness of an artist's world and the idiosyncratic features of his language is thus no excuse for lack of explication of that world as revealed in what he has actually written. Nor is a confessed hermeneutic genesis of some interpretation a proof of its validity. Even Kafka's world—if accessible at all—is accessible via potentialities inherent in ordinary language. And any interpretation, whether of fiction or fact, is bound to some residual shared social reality or presupposed commonality with respect to interpretation. The MAN in Kipling's poem 'If', for instance, is thus neither an idiosyncratic inhabitant of the author's imaginary world nor even a uniquely poetic creature, but perfectly comprehensible in terms of semantic potentialities of the word as revealed in ordinary usage. He is certainly different from the MAN in an utterance such as (V I), p. 108, yet similar to MAN in other contexts of everyday discourse (see Rommetveit 1972c, pp. 64 and 94–7) such as:

(V U) He had indeed proved he was a MAN,

(V V) That was a MAN's job,

and

(V W) The kitchen was a mess. It was easy to see that a MAN had been there.

And the resemblance cannot be assessed in terms of any unequivocally shared and autonomous emotive feature, since being Kipling's MAN is worth more than being in possession of the entire earth, whereas the poor MAN in (V W) is inferred on that basis of a messy kitchen. The *Why* of communication and the reciprocally endorsed presuppositions are in all these cases such, however, that potentialities of purely zoological taxonomy are eliminated. The manhood of MAN must hence in every case be described in terms of sex role attribution[13] rather than categorization of species, sex and age, yet in each particular case as bound to a different *temporarily* shared social reality.

The hermeneutic scholar tends in his interpretation to maximize such residual social realities, and a claim that he has 'seized upon the right interpretation' is made with reference to 'potentialities of human experience' and 'a wider meaning which is composed of language and the practice of living'. His explication of 'the real meaning' is accordingly addressed to us as insiders of a presumedly universal, though entirely open and undefined '*Interpretations-gemeinschaft*'. *Semanticists of the Harvard–M.I.T. school, on the other hand, are concerned with 'literal' rather than literary meanings, with synonymy salva veritate rather than possible worlds, and with invariant semantic features rather than semantic potentialities.* Residuals other than those of an axiomatic nature are therefore only reluctantly dealt with and—when acknowledged at all—dealt with primarily as deviations from fully determined propositional content. The myth of *an art of literary interpretation* as opposed to *a science of general semantics* is thus firmly rooted in encapsulated academic traditions based upon divergent, even though largely unexplored, philosophical premises.

We have in preceding chapters tried to explore significant residuals of human communication in terms of premises for intersubjectivity such as *complementarity, capacities for decentered categorization and attribution,* and *a capacity to adapt the perspectives of different 'others'.* The temporarily shared social world of the dialogue may be explored in terms of partially shared cognitive–emotive perspectives, and what is made known has to be described in terms of expansions and/or modification of such an intersubjectively established social world. Semantic potentialities must within such a conceptual framework be conceived of as linguistically mediated drafts of contracts concerning categorization and attribution, bound to more comprehensive schemes, yet to a considerable extent negotiable and contingent upon meta-contracts and pre-established or actively induced '*sous-entendus*'. And contextually determined 'word meanings'—whether 'literal' or 'literary', 'matter-of-fact' orientated or 'metaphorical'—must hence in an analysis of message structure be dealt with as manifestations of common semantic potentialities bound to variant premises for intersubjectivity.

VI

EPILOGUE: ON INTERSUBJECTIVITY ACROSS ACADEMIC BOUNDARIES

IRRATIONAL compartmentalization of knowledge is sustained by vicious circles, and obvious shortcomings of encapsulated academic traditions may even lead to further subdivision and novel fields of specialization. The *raison d'être* of a separate hermeneutic expertise on literary exceptions must thus in part be sought in an encapsulated semantic expertise on general rules for 'literal readings'—and *vice versa*.[14] A programmatic disregard of problems of language use within the Harvard–M.I.T. school of structural linguistics, moreover, has recently been replaced by a rapidly increasing interest in pragmatics: the paradigms for assessing propositional form and content for sentences *in vacuo* have, as we have seen, been expanded and modified so as to cope with 'readings' of utterances encountered in variant extralinguistic settings.

What is made known in acts of verbal communication, however, cannot be properly assessed by a mere extrapolation from propositional analysis of the sentence *in vacuo* to extraneously assessed conditions of use. The conceptual framework outlined in this book has therefore been elaborated in explicit opposition to such a development: what is made known by any given verbal expression—whether 'literal' or 'metaphorical'—has been explored as bound by meta-contracts of communication explicitly or tactily endorsed by the participants engaged in that particular act of communication, and common semantic potentialities have been conceived of as drafts of contracts concerning shared strategies of categorization and attribution.

Message potentials, moreover, have been pondered in terms of alternative possible and plausible premises for intersubjectivity and—for each such alternative—against the background of alternative constellations of presuppositions. The subtle interplay between meta-contracts, presuppositions and what is actually written or said has accordingly been explored within the framework of the dialogue.

Procedures for assessing message structure may for that reason eventually be formalized in accordance with paradigms for logical analysis such as Lorenzen's '*dialogical tables*' (Lorenzen 1967). What is asserted by the speaker is in his tables revealed in terms of potential objections by a critical listener, and general rules of logical debate are defined in contracts endorsed by both participants. Such rules make it possible to decide, at any stage, (1) whether the debate has been terminated and, if that is the case, (2) who has 'won'. What is asserted, morever, may by contract, be defined in terms of truth values or in terms of particular procedures for verification.

Some of the residuals we have ended up with in preceding analyses of message structure may indeed very plausibly be further explicated in terms of *what may be said next*. Partial determination of expressions and optional elaborations of general drafts of contracts may hence, in accordance with Lorenzen's paradigm, be translated into formal criteria for explicating possible continuations of a dialogue and/or tacitly accepted procedures for proof.

It is doubtful, however, how much can be gained by such attempts at formalization. Our insight into architectures of intersubjectivity is as yet of a very fragmentary nature, and the field of structural linguistics is replete with premature formalizations. A common basis for humanistic and social scientific studies of language can only be established if we are willing to broaden our perspective and engage in radical revaluations of existing subdivisions and current paradigms for research. What is needed at the present stage is thus neither additional formal devices nor more subdisciplines, but a more comprehensive and thorough analysis of basic premises for intersubjectivity and contractual aspects of verbal communication.

What has been said about residuals in human communication in this book may therefore be applied recursively: I am, in retrospect, painfully aware of unresolved ambiguities in the preceding accounts of architectures of intersubjectivity, message structures and semantic potentialities. Let me hence briefly, but true to my main objective, indicate how *some* such residual ambiguities may be further illuminated in dialogues across academic boundaries and serve as points of departure for novel theoretical and empirical inquiries.

Consider, first, what has been said about *variant realizations of common semantic potentialities*. Semantic potentialities can in acts of verbal communication only be identified indirectly, against the background of some residual, yet specified commonality with respect to interpretation. And even tacit residuals of an axiomatic nature may vary from one situation to another: the manhood of MAN may on one occasion be intended and understood in terms of a biologically defined dichotomy and on another occasion in terms of sex role attribution.

The latter potentiality is in dictionary accounts of our common code and in current semantic treatises only *'sous-entendu'* and—at most—dealt with in small letters on the reverse of documents prescribing 'literal use'. It is contingent upon categorization of biological sex, yet *bound to a man-made social reality*. What is tacitly presupposed about women and men in sex role prescriptions in everyday interaction, moreover, may be revealed in 'selection restrictions' on other nouns with which the words WOMAN and MAN form compounds (see Blakar 1974). The commonality with respect to interpretation may also be mirrored in maps of semantic–associative networks based upon word sorting and word associations (Rommetveit 1972c, pp. 60–7). Additional insight into significant potentialities of words such as WOMAN and MAN in everyday and literary use may hence be achieved by convergent linguistic, sociological and psychological inquiries, since what is made known by those words in acts of communication is bound to more inclusive and behaviourally mastered strategies of attribution.

Creative transcendence of conventional use, moreover, may possibly be explored in terms of novel patterns of dependency among familiar semantic potentialities. The sex role manhood of MAN is hardly ever more unequivocally intended and understood than in apparent contradictions and tautologies such as, for example, 'That woman is a MAN' and 'That man is really a MAN', i.e. when what might otherwise be made known about biological sex is either clearly *overruled* or obviously *redundant*. And we have shown in our analysis of the word INFANT in particular contexts how alternative conventional metaphorical potentialities are brought into action, depending upon what in each particular act of communication is already assumed to be the case.

Most novel metaphors appear at first glance blatantly contradictory: some entity X is claimed to be a Y—my CURIOSITY is an OCEAN; my THOUGHTS are SHIPS—and whatever is made known by such a claim is clearly contingent upon a firmly shared conviction that X is *not* Y.

The semantic potentialities operant in such metaphorical contexts are obviously bound to commonalities with respect to interpretation transcending those elaborated in geographical definitions and technical dictionaries. They are common semantic potentialities inherent in words such as OCEAN and SHIP, however, clearly reflected as fringe potentialities in maps of semantic–associative networks (see Rommetveit 1968a, pp. 257–63, and 1972c, p. 95), and as much part of ordinary language as semantic features elaborated in technical dictionaries.[15] Such potentialities must therefore be conceived of as potentially shared cognitive–emotive perspectives of an anthropomorphic nature, perfectly admissible within an anthropocentrically based semantics or, in Greimas' terms, within *'une lexématisme anthropocentrique'* (Greimas 1966, p. 56). The metaphors presented above may thus, for instance in a particular poetic context, be understood as conveying the idea that my curiosity is deep and inexplorable, whereas my thoughts—carried by my curiosity—are mobile and bound for particular destinations.

My curiosity and *an ocean* are in such a case introduced by linguistic means into a temporarily shared social world and attended to as similar in some respect. A particular decentered perspective is accordingly induced by a particular constellation of semantic potentialities: abstract and only partially determined potentialities of OCEAN such as, for example, *depth* and *inexplorability* are brought into focus because otherwise salient potentialities referring to less abstract attributes are overruled. And the resultant cognitive perspective may even represent a genuinely novel categorization as far as the adult reader of the poem is concerned. Even if that should be the case, it is immediately mastered on the basis of his intuitive mastery of the word OCEAN.

The *depth* and *inexplorability* potentialities of OCEAN may be brought into focus in a variety of other metaphorical constellations as well such as 'My GRIEF (LOVE, GUILT, DESÍRE, etc.) is an OCEAN'. Common semantic potentialities may thus be revealed in systematic investigations of metaphors, and the mysteries of creative transcendence of conventional use may be explored in terms of what we know about similar, but more conventional, linguistically mediated categorizations. The resemblance between *my curiosity* and *an ocean* implied in a poetic context appears to be of the same kind as that between *to die* and *to sleep* brought into focus in Hamlet's monologue (see p. 118). It is in principle hardly any more mysterious, however, than that between *John* and *a typewriter* implied in fragments of everyday conversation such as 'John is so EASY to handle; he has become nothing but an INSTRU-MENT for his boss' (see p. 26). What is made known is in either case contingent upon contracts concerning abstract categorizations inherent in ordinary language and—*eo ipso*—upon our capacities for decentered shifts of perspectives in communication about a multifaceted social world.

Further investigation of metaphors may thus be planned as a joint venture by general semanticists in search of *common semantic potentialities*, students of literature concerned with *creative transcendence* of conventional language use, and psychologists inquiring into abstract thought and *decentered categorization*. Metaphors are never encountered *in vacuo*, however, but are—as we have shown—bound to institutionally determined and/or situationally induced premises for intersubjectivity. A general semanticist whose expertise pertains to interpretation of scientific texts and a hermeneutically trained student of poetry will thus, once engaged in a joint venture, become seriously concerned about variant premises for intersubjectivity. And our hypothetical transplantations of texts in Chapter IV. 2 may in that case serve as a point of departure for more systematic comparative studies.

The various patterns of dependencies we have encountered in analysis of message structure, moreover, may possibly be further illuminated in dialogues between psychologists engaged in research on *comprehensibility* and scholars concerned with aspects of *literary style*. Comprehensibility is thus, in view of recent psycholinguistic experiments on the effects of different optional word orders on recall, to a large extent a matter of isomorphy between message structure and temporal organization of speech (Wold 1971, Jaspars *et al.* 1971, Rommetveit 1972c, pp. 132–43). And such an isomorphy may indeed prove a necessity in communication with the mentally retarded child, since most forms of retardation are characterized by deficient capacity to store semantic potentialities in expectation of subsequently provided premises for interpretation. Making things known to the seriously retarded child is thus possible only by means of a strictly step-wise progressive expansion of a very restricted perceptual and social reality.

The potential relevance of such psycholinguistic studies of comprehensibility for analysis of style has been suggested in our discussion of prolepsis and anticipatory comprehension. *Strict isomorphy between message structure and temporal sequence of what is said or written allows for cumulative decoding*: the premises for making full sense of what is said have at each stage already been provided by the speaker, the listener is *not* forced to engage in prolepsis, and his listening is accordingly devoid of the suspense and adventure of potential deceptive anticipatory comprehension.

Discrepancy between message structure and temporal order, on the other hand, makes for prolepsis and—at times—even for intentionally deceptive anticipatory comprehension. What is taken for granted by the reader of a short story when he makes sense of one particular passage may thus be contradicted by premises made known to him on the following page. And precisely such a state of affairs may be intended by the author: he knows, by anticipatory decoding, what will be taken for granted, and *his contradiction of a conventionally adopted perspective, is made known against the background of a deceptive confirmation.*

What is 'understood backward' in such a case is clearly dependent upon less than perfect initial complementarity, since that which is intended by the author is not at all presupposed by his reader to be so intended. And we may ask: is such initial lack of complementarity generally the case in human communication resulting in *transcendence* rather than mere *expansion* of a pre-established social reality?

The difficulties we encounter when we engage in dialogues across traditional academic boundaries should, if that is the case, carry promises of creative transcendence.

NOTES

1. 'Dogma' is in the case actually used in the way Kant conceived of religious dogmas, i.e. as assumed prerequisites for hope (see Buber 1962, p. 689).
2. I have personally noticed present tense used by Midwesterners in response to precisely such questions. Such use is, of course, also spontaneously understood and can hence hardly be considered ungrammatical, even though the progressive 'I am thinking' may be by far the most frequently employed form on such occasions within most dialects of English. Present tense will be perfectly acceptable, moreover, if the speaker is making known his *thought* as opposed to, for example, his *hope*. The word 'think' in (II D) may thus be stressed when the whole utterance is preceded by 'I *hope* my son will stay away from every kind of drug, but . . .'.
3. The speaker (son of the labour minister) is a radical Brazilian student.
4. X, X' and X" represent what is talked *about*. Y stands for 'an artist' and Z for 'a person'. In this way, the apparent contradiction between 'yes' at stage (1) and 'don't know' at stage (3) is avoided in the transcription.
5. An example of dual relevance in the present context is the Edinburgh Conference on Psycholinguistics in 1966. It is in retrospect quite amusing to notice how difficult it was for 'outsiders' at that conference to engage in communication with proponents of the Harvard–M.I.T. school on premises other than those based upon faith in 'deep syntactic structures', premises that no longer are agreed upon *within* the Harvard–M.I.T. school (see Lyons and Wales 1966, Rommetveit 1968b).
6. The resultant immediate 'disambiguation' is hence analogous to effects of verbally induced sets on perception of ambiguous figures and to context effects upon resolution of binocular rivalry of letters.
7. Notice, however, how the tacit agreement concerning what constitutes old age in this particular context differs from what may be presupposed in a similar conversation between two very old men about a newcomer to the home for old people in which they are living. The genuinely contractual aspect of 'old' in the context of 'old people' is thus revealed in optional elaborations of the same general semantic potentiality.
8. Such a range of plausible situations, however, must be described in terms of alternative sets of premises for intersubjectivity rather than as representative of some undefined 'standard contract'.
9. Consider, for instance, the following situation. A fairly young lady is asked whether she too is constantly criticized by her children, and she responds 'My only child is fortunately still an INFANT'. What is made known by the word on that occasion appears indeed to be mediated by a semantic potentiality corresponding to its etymologically 'literal' meaning, namely *incapacity to speak*.
10. Consider, on the other hand, how the *animate potentiality* is overruled in utterances such as, for example, 'Our programme for adult education is still an INFANT'. *Stage of life cycle* potentialities are in such a case *eo ipso* detached from biological life and bound to periodicity having to do with institutional growth and decay.
11. The CAN explored by Heider in his analysis of personal causality is thus *not* the CAN of modal logic. The latter CAN will not be discussed at all in the present work, but its relationship to Lakoff's 'natural logic' of CAN has been cogently analysed by Barth (1974).

12. The dependency of DIE upon attribution of personal causality may be further illuminated if we ponder what may be made known by the verb in a robot society. Familiar *legal* aspects of DIE such as *termination of personal responsibility* would in such a society be utterly incomprehensible.

13. Sex role attribution is by no means an issue of relevance only to the semantics of WOMAN and MAN and related words, compounds and derivatives, but even revealed as prolepsis in nonreflective use of reflexive pronouns. Notice, for instance, the tacit inference from 'one' (the 'generalized linguist') to 'himself' in the following excerpt from *a treatise on reflexives:*

> (McCawley 1972, p. 504) Evidently, the possibility of using a reflexive depends on whether *one avails himself* of the option provided by English grammar of moving the subject of certain subordinate clauses into the main clause. (Italics mine)

14. See Chomsky's 'reading' of the word UNCLE, p. 18.
15. See our brief discussion of 'scientific dialects', p. 20.

REFERENCES

Apel, K. O. (1965). Die Entfaltung der 'sprachanalytischen' Philosophie und das Problem der 'Geisteswissenschaft', *Philos. Jahrbuch*, **72**, 239–89.

Apel, K. O. (1966). Wittegenstein und das Problem des hermeneutischen Verstehens, *Zeitschrift für Teologie und Kirche*, **63**, 49–87.

Apel, K. O. (1968). Szientifik, Hermeneutik, Ideologie-Kritik: Entwerf einer Wissenschaftslehre in erkenntnis-anthropologischen Sicht, *Man and the World*, **I**, 37–68.

Aubert, V. (1958). Legal justice and mental health, *Psychiatry*, **21**, 101–13.

Barth, E. M. (1974). Untimely remarks on the logic of 'the modalities' in natural language. In C. Heidrich (Ed.) *Semantics and Communication*, North-Holland, Amsterdam, in press.

Bateson, G. (1955). A theory of play and fantasy, *Psychiatric Research Reports*, **2**, 39–51.

Bateson, G., Jackson, D. D., Haley, J., and Weakland, J. (1956). Toward a theory of schizophrenia, *Behavioral Science*, **1**, 251–64.

Berger, P. L., and Luckmann, T. (1967). *The Construction of Social Reality*, Doubleday, New York.

Bever, T. G. (1970). The cognitive bases for linguistic structures, In J. R. Hayes (Ed.), *Cognition and the Development of Language*, Wiley, New York, pp. 279–362.

Bierwisch, M. (1971). Poetik och lingvistik, In K. Aspelin and B. A. Lundberg (Eds.), *Form och Struktur*, PAN/Norstedts, Stockholm, pp. 187–217.

Birdwhistell, R. L. (1971). *Kinesics and Context*, Allan Lane, London.

Blakar, R. M. (1974). Language as a means of social power, In J. Mey (Ed.), *Studies in Pragmatic Linguistics*, Mouton, The Hague, In press.

Blakar, R. M., and Rommetveit, R. (1974). Utterances *in vacuo* and in contexts: an experimental and theoretical exploration of some interrelationships between what is heard and what is seen or imagined, *International J. Psycholinguistics*, In press.

Brown, R., and Gilman, A. (1966). The pronouns of power and solidarity, In A. Sebeok, *Style in Language*, M.I.T. Press, Cambridge, Mass.

Bråten, S. (1973). Coding simulation circuits during symbolic interaction, Paper at *7th International Congress on Cybernetics*, Namur.

Buber, M. (1962). What is Man? In W. Barrett and H. E. Aiken (Eds.), *Philosophy in the Twentieth Century*, vol. **4**, Random House, New York, pp. 688–719.

Chafe, W. (1970). *Meaning and the Structure of Language*, University of Chicago Press, Chicago.

Chomsky, N. (1957). *Syntactic Structures*, Mouton, The Hague.

Chomsky, N. (1965). *Aspects of a Theory of Syntax*, M.I.T. Press, Cambridge, Mass.

Chomsky, N. (1968). *Language and Mind*, Harcourt, Brace & World, New York.

Chomsky, N. (1972). *Studies on Semantics in Generative Grammar*, Mouton, The Hague.

Cohen, L. J., and Margalit, A. (1972). The role of inductive reasoning in the interpretation of metaphor, In D. Davidson and G. Harman (Eds.), *Semantics of Natural Language*, Reidel, Dordrecht, pp. 722–40.

Corvéz, M. (1969). *Les Structuralistes*, Aubier-Montaigne, Paris.

Ducrot, O. (1972). *Dire et ne pas dire. Principes de Semantique linguistique*, Hermann, Paris.

132

Ervin-Tripp, S. M., and Slobin, D. (1966). Psycholinguistics, *Annual Review of Psychology*, **17**, 435–74.

Festinger, L. (1954). A theory of social comparison processes, *Human Relations*, **7**, 117–40.

Fillmore, C. J. (1972). Subjects, speakers and roles, In D. Davidson and G. Harman (Eds.), *Semantics of Natural Language*, Reidel, Dordrecht, pp. 1–24.

Frege, G. (1969). *Funktion, Begriff, Bedeutung*, ed. G. Patzig, Vandenhoeck & Ruprecht, Göttingen.

Gleason, H. A. jr. (1968). Contrastive analysis in discourse structure, *Monograph Series on Language and Linguistics*, ed. J. E. Alatis, no. 21, 39–63, University Press, Georgetown.

Greimas, A. J. (1966). *Semantique Structurale*, Librarie Larousse, Paris.

Habermas, J. (1968). *Erkenntnis und Interesse*, Suhrkamp, Frankfurt a.M.

Hebb, D. C. (1946). Emotion in Man and Animal: an analysis of the intuitive processes of recognition, *Psychol. Rev.*, **53**, 88–106.

Heider, F. (1958). *The Psychology of Interpersonal Relations*, Wiley, New York.

Hemingway, E. (1970). *A Moveable Feast*, Bantam Books, New York.

Hull, C. L. (1920). *Quantitative Aspects of the Evolution of Concepts: An Experimental Study*. Psychol. Monogr., **28**, no. 1.

Husserl, E. (1962). Consciousness and natural reality, In W. Barret and H. D. Aiken (Eds.), *Philosophy in the Twentieth Century*, vol. 3, Random House, New York, pp. 179–205.

Husserl, E. (1964). *The Phenomenology of Internal Time Consciousness*, Martinus Nijhoff, The Hague.

Jakobson, R. (1966). Linguistics and poetics, In T. A. Sebeok (Ed.), *Style in Language*, M.I.T. Press, Cambridge, Mass.

Jaspars, J., Rommetveit, R., Cook, M., Havelka, N., Henry, P., Herkner, W., Pêcheux, M., and Peeters, G. (1971). Order effects in impression formation: A psycholinguistic approach, In E. A. Carswell and R. Rommetveit (Eds.), *Social Contexts of Messages*, Academic Press, London.

Just, M., Carpenter, P. (1971). Comprehension of negation with quantification, *J. Verb. Learn. Beh.*, **10**, 244–53.

Katz, J. J., and Fodor, J. A. (1963). The structure of a semantic theory, *Language*, **39**, 170–210.

Kelly, G. A. (1955). *The Psychology of Personal Constructs*, Norton, New York.

Krech, D., and Cruchfield, R. S. (1966). *Elements of Psychology*, Knopf, New York.

Kuhn, T. S. (1970). The structure of scientific revolutions, *International Encyclopedia of Unified Science*, vol. II, no. 2, University of Chicago Press, Chicago.

Lakoff, G. (1972). Linguistics and natural logic, In D. Davidson and G. Harman (Eds.), *Semantics of Natural Language*, Reidel, Dordrecht, pp. 545–665.

Lane, H., and Tranel, B. (1971). The Lombard sign and the role of hearing in speech, *J. of Speech and Hearing Research*, **14**, 677–709.

Lashley, K. S. (1951). The problem of serial order in behaviour, In L. A. Jeffress (Ed.), *Cerebral Mechanisms in Behavior*, Wiley, New York, pp. 112–36.

Leeper, R. W. (1935). A study of a neglected portion of the field of learning: the development of sensory organization, *J. Genet. Psychol.*, **46**, 41–75.

Levin, S. R. (1971). Poesi och grammatikalitet, In K. Aspelin and B. A. Lundberg (Eds.), *Form och Struktur*, PAN/Norstedts, Stockholm, pp. 179–86.

Lévi-Strauss, C. (1964). Structural analysis in linguistics and anthropology, In D. Hymes (Ed.), *Language in Culture and Society*, Harper & Row, New York, pp. 40–53.

Lévi-Strauss, C. (1971). *L'Homme Nu*, Plon, Paris.

Liberman, A. M., Cooper, F. S., Shankweiler, D. P., and Studdert-Kennedy, M. (1967). Perception of the speech code, *Psychol. Rev.*, **74**, 431–61.

133

Lorenzen, P. (1967). *Métamathématique*, Mouton, Paris.

Lotman, J. (1971). Teser till problemet 'Konstens plats bland de modellbildande systemen', In K. Aspelin and B. A. Lundberg (Eds.), *Form och Struktur*, PAN/Norstedts, Stockholm, pp. 281–99.

Lyons, J., and Wales, R. J. (Eds.) (1966). *Psycholinguistic Papers*, University of Edinburgh Press, Edinburgh.

Malcolm, N. (1967). *Ludwig Wittgenstein. A Memoir*, Oxford University Press, London.

McCawley, J. D. (1972). A program for logic, In D. Davidson and G. Harman (Eds.), *Semantics of Natural Language*, Reidel, Dordrecht, pp. 498–544.

Mead, G. H. (1950). *Mind, Self, and Society from the Standpoint of a Behaviorist*, University of Chicago Press, Chicago.

Merleau-Ponty, M. (1962). *Phenomenology of Perception*, Routledge & Kegan Paul, London.

Michotte, A. (1954). *La Perception de la Causalité*, Publications Universitaires de Louvain, Louvain.

Miller, G. A. (1953). What is in formation measurement?, *American Psychologist*, **8**, 3–11.

Miller, G. A. (1962). Some psychological studies of grammar, *American Psychologist*, **17**, 748–62.

Miller, G. A. (1969). A psychological method to investigate verbal concepts, *J. Math. Psychol.*, **6**, 169–91.

Miller, G. A., Galanter, E., and Pribram, K. H. (1960). *Plans and the Structure of Behavior*, Holt, New York.

Miller, G. A., and McNeill, D. (1969). Psycholinguistics, In G. Lindzey and E. Aronson (Eds.), *Handbook of Social Psychology*, vol. III, pp. 666–794.

Miller, G. A., and Selfridge, J. (1950). Verbal context and the recall of meaningful material, *Amer. J. Psychol.*, **63**, 176–85.

Moscovici, S., and Plon, M. (1966). Les situations colloques, *Bulletin de Psychologie*, **19**, 702–22.

Mukařovský, J. (1971). Strukturalismen i estetiken och i litteraturvetenskapen, In K. Aspelin and B. A. Lundberg (Eds.), *From och Struktur*, PAN/Norstedts, Stockholm, pp. 127–47.

Noble, C. E. (1952). The role of stimulus meaning (m) in serial verbal learning, *J. Exp. Psychol.*, **49**, 333–8.

Osgood, C. E. (1962). Studies on the generality of affective meaning systems, *American Psychologist*, **7**, 10–28.

Piaget, J. (1926). *The Language and Thought of the Child*, Harcourt & Brace, New York.

Piaget, J. (1952). *The Origin of Intelligence in Children*, International University Press, New York.

Piaget, J. (1968). *Le Structuralisme*, Presses Universitaires de France, Paris.

Prûcha, J. (1972). Psycholinguistics and Sociolinguistics—separate or integrated?, *International J. of Psycholinguistics*, **1**, 9–23.

Quine, W. V. (1961). *Word and Object*, Wiley, New York.

Quine, W. V. (1972). Methodological reflections on current linguistic theory, In D. Davidson and G. Harman (Eds.), *Semantics of Natural Language*, Reidel, Dordrecht, pp. 442–54.

Reddy, M. J. (1969). A semantic approach to metaphors, In R. I. Binnick *et al.* (Eds.), Papers from the Fifth Annual Meeting of Chicago Linguistic Society, University of Chicago, pp. 205–39.

Reichling, A. (1963). Das Problem der Bedeutung in der Sprachwissenschaft, *Innsbrucker Beiträge zur Kulturwissenschaft*, Sonderheft **19**.

Rommetveit, R. (1953). *Social Norms and Roles*, Universitetsforlaget, Oslo.

134

Rommetveit, R. (1958). *Ego i moderne psykologi*, Universitetsforlaget, Oslo.
Rommetveit, R. (1960a), *Selectivity, Intuition and Halo Effects in Social Perception*, Universitetsforlaget, Oslo.
Rommetveit, R. (1960b), *Action and Ideation*, Munksgaard, Copenhagen.
Rommetveit, R. (1968a), *Words, Meanings and Messages*, Academic Press and Universitetsforlaget, New York and Oslo.
Rommetveit, R. (1968b), Review of J. Lyons and R. J. Wales (Eds.), Psycholinguistic Papers, *Lingua*, **19**, 305–11.
Rommetveit, R. (1970). Verbal communication and social influence, In J. R. Wittenborn *et al.* (Eds.), *Communication and Drug Abuse*, Charles C. Thomas, Springfield, pp. 69–78.
Rommetveit, R. (1971). On concepts of hierarchical structures and micro-analysis of language and thought, In G. Eckblad (Ed.), *Hierarchical Models in the Study of Cognition*, Institute of Psychology, Bergen.
Rommetveit, R. (1972a), Language games, deep syntactic structures, and hermeneutic circles, In J. Israel and H. Taifel (Eds.), *The Context of Social Psychology: A Critical Assessment*, Academic Press, London, pp. 212–57.
Rommetveit, R. (1972b), Deep structure of sentences versus message structure. Some critical remarks on current paradigms, and suggestions for an alternative approach, *Norwegian J. of Linguistics*, **26**, 3–22.
Rommetveit, R. (1972c), *Språk, tanke og kommunikasjon. Ei innføring i språkpsykologi og psykolingvistikk*, Universitetsforlaget, Oslo.
Rommetveit, R., and Blakar, R. M. (1973). Induced semantic–associative states and resolution of binocular rivalry conflicts between letters, *Scand. J. Psychol.*, **14**, 185–94.
Rommetveit, R., Cook, M., Havelka, N., Henry, P., Herkner, W., Pêcheux, M., and Peeters, G. (1971). Processing of utterances in context, In E. A. Carswell and R. Rommetveit (Eds.), *Social Contexts of Messages*, Academic Press, London, pp. 29–56.
Rommetveit, R., and Kvale, S. (1965a), Stages in concept formation. III. Further inquiries into an extra intention to verbalize, *Scand. J. Psychol.*, **6**, 65–74.
Rommetveit, R., and Kvale, S. (1965b), Stages in concept formation. IV. A temporal analysis of effects of an extra intention to verbalize, *Scand. J. Psychol.*, **6**, 75–9.
Rossi, I. (1973). The unconscious in the anthropology of Claude Lévi–Strauss, *Amer. Anthropologist*, **75**, 20–48.
Russell, B. (1940). *Inquiry into Meaning and Truth*, Allen, London.
Schachter, S., and Singer, J. E. (1962). Cognitive, social and physiological determinants of emotive state, *Psychol. Rev.*, **69**, 379–99.
Shannon, C. E. (1951). Prediction and entropy of printed English, *Bell System Technical Journal*, **30**, 50–64.
Šklovskij, V. (1971). Konsten som grepp, In K. Aspelin and B. A. Lundberg (Eds.), *Form och Struktur*, PAN/Norstedts, Stockholm, pp. 45–63.
Smedslund, J. (1964). *Concrete Reasoning: A Study of Intellectual Development. Monographs of the Society for Research in Child Development*, **29**, no. 2.
Stalnaker, R. C. (1972). Pragmatics, In D. Davidson and G. Harman (Eds.), *Semantics of Natural Language*, Reidel, Dordrecht, pp. 380–97.
Strawson, P. F. (1964). Identifying reference and truth-values, *Theoria*, **30**, 96–118.
Strawson, P. F. (1969). *Individuals*, Methuen, London.
Turner, E. A., and Rommetveit, R. (1967a), The acquisition of sentence voice and reversibility, *Child Development*, **38**, 649–60.
Turner, E. A., and Rommetveit, R. (1967b), Experimental manipulation of the production of active and passive voice in children, *Language and Speech*, **10**, 169–80.
Uhlenbeck, E. M. (1963). An appraisal of transformation theory, *Lingua*, **12**, 1–18.

Urmson, J. C. (1963). Parenthetical verbs, In C. E. Caton (Ed.), *Philosophy and Ordinary Language*, University of Illinois Press, Urbana.

Valery, P. (1951). *Essays og Aforismer*, G. Mortensens forlag, Oslo.

Vygotsky, L. S. (1962). *Thought and Language*, Wiley, New York.

Watzlawick, P., Beavin, J. H., and Jackson, D. D. (1967). *Pragmatics of Human Communication. A study of interactional patterns, pathologies, and paradoxes*, Norton, New York.

Weinreich, U. (1963). On the semantic structure of language, In J. H. Greenberg (Ed.), *Universals of Language*, M.I.T. Press, Cambridge, Mass.

Wellek, R. (1966). From the point of view of literary criticism. Closing statement, In T. A. Sebeok (Ed.), *Style in Language*, M.I.T. Press, Cambridge, Mass.

Wittgenstein, L. (1922). *Tractatus Logico-Philosophicus*, Routledge & Kegan Paul, London.

Wittgenstein, L. (1961). *Note Books* (Ed. G. H. von Wright and G. E. M. Anscombe), Harper & Row, New York.

Wittgenstein, L. (1962). The Blue Book, In W. Barret and H. D. Aiken (Eds.), *Philosophy in the Twentieth Century*, vol. 2, Random House, New York, pp. 710–74.

Wittgenstein, L. (1968). *Philosophische Untersuchungen—Philosophical Investigations* (Ed. G. E. Anscombe), Blackwell, Oxford.

Wold, A. H. (1971). Impression formation: A psycholinguistic approach. Progress report, In E. A. Carswell and R. Rommetveit (Eds.), *Social Contexts of Messages*, Academic Press, London, pp. 127–38.

NAME INDEX

138

SUBJECT INDEX

142